Praise for *Small Business Revolution*

"The cornerstone of Deluxe has always been the success of small business. As the landscape of the world continually changes, Deluxe adapts and evolves to keep that as their top priority, bringing innovative ways for these businesses to survive and ultimately thrive. The tapestry of America would be far less colorful if we don't all work to keep this part of our country alive and well."

—Ty Pennington,
renovation icon, TV personality

"Small business owners need this book now more than ever. There are few things more rewarding and more challenging than running a small business, and Barry McCarthy and his team at Deluxe are proven experts at how to do it. This comprehensive book will help you improve your game and successfully deal with the challenges small business leaders have always faced as well as the new challenges created by Covid and seismic change. I recommend it."

—Mark Sanborn,
award-winning speaker and bestselling
author of *The Fred Factor* and
You Don't Need a Title to be a Leader;
President of Sanborn & Associates

"Powerful curation insights every entrepreneur and their allies need to understand."

—Ramon Ray,
founder, SmartHustle.com;
Entrepreneur in Residence,
Oracle NetSuite

"Every day, entrepreneurs take the plunge to start their own business, taking a life's passion and turning it into a dream. With *Small Business Revolution*, Barry McCarthy showcases what it takes to succeed in an ever-changing world, while providing tangible, practical examples of business owners who are doing it every day. Few books capture the spirit of the business owner like this one does."

—Katie Kirkpatrick,
President and CEO,
Metro Atlanta Chamber of Commerce

"Barry's book is a reliable roadmap for the business builder and lifelong learner in all of us. It's a quality series of best practices from a fellow CEO who has clearly listened to and responded to the small business community. Entrepreneurial life is not for everyone, but if it is your path of joy Barry can help you find practices to better face the adversity and chaos inherent in new ventures."

—Ryan Millsap,
Entrepreneur in Entertainment, Real Estate,
and Private Equity Industries, Chairman and CEO
of the Blackhall Group, founder of Blackhall Studios

"This book is full of insights and stories from the head of a company that's been in business for over a century. Barry's book will nourish you with the resources and resilience to make it big in the small business world."

—Michael J. Coles,
cofounder of the Great American Cookie Company,
former CEO of Caribou Coffee, and author of *Time to Get Tough:
How Cookies, Coffee, and a Crash Led to Success in Business and Life*

"These are challenging times for small business owners and this book helps those owners navigate these uncharted waters. With his commonsense approach, Barry charts a course for success, helping entrepreneurs understand how to better position their business, reach new customers, and understand when it is time to ask for help."

—Charlie Weaver,
Executive Director, Minnesota Business Partnership

"As a founder of several small businesses and a current small business co-owner, I know first-hand the value that these business owners bring to every community and the country. This book captures the challenges and triumphs of being a small business owner with specific examples and insights from a company that has been helping small businesses for more than 100 years."

—Cheryl Mayberry McKissack,
President and co-owner of Black Opal LLC, founder and CEO of
Nia Enterprises, LLC; Chair, Deluxe Corporation

"Small businesses are the lifeblood of communities. They employ our friends and neighbors. The tips and tools that Barry and Deluxe have amassed over the past 106 years can help entrepreneurs learn how to grow their businesses and reach new audiences."

—Keith Ferrazzi,
American entrepreneur, recognized global thought leader and *New York Times*
bestselling author of *Who's Got Your Back* and *Never Eat Alone*

BARRY C. McCARTHY

CEO, DELUXE

Small

BUSINESS

REVOLUTION

HOW OWNERS AND ENTREPRENEURS
CAN SUCCEED

WILEY

Published by John Wiley & Sons, Inc., Hoboken, New Jersey.
Published simultaneously in Canada.

For general information on our other products and services or for technical support, please contact our Customer Care Department within the United States at (800) 762-2974, outside the United States at (317) 572-3993 or fax (317) 572-4002.

Wiley publishes in a variety of print and electronic formats and by print-on-demand. Some material included with standard print versions of this book may not be included in e-books or in print-on-demand. If this book refers to media such as a CD or DVD that is not included in the version you purchased, you may download this material at http://booksupport.wiley.com. For more information about Wiley products, visit www.wiley.com.

Library of Congress Cataloging-in-Publication Data is Available:

ISBN 9781119802648 (Hardback)
ISBN 9781119802655 (ePDF)
ISBN 9781119802662 (ePub)

Cover Design: Wiley
Cover Image: © MicrovOne/Getty Images

SKY10029059_081221

To my fellow Deluxers, for always having the grit and perseverance to put customers first, helping small businesses succeed, for more than 100 years.

To my beautiful wife, Jean Ann. You have always been my rock and my inspiration, my partner, my best friend, and you have always encouraged me to strive-to help others succeed. Thank you.

To my amazing children, Will, Matt, and Katie, who put up with a dedicated businessman and committed community leader as a father.

To my parents and in-laws, Tom & Lori McCarthy and Ron & Mary Ann Hood, teachers and small businesspeople, who taught me about faith, integrity, the dignity of labor, the importance of hard work, and perseverance—to always believe in yourself, and to never, ever give up.

Contents

Introduction

In Taking on this endeavor, I thought a lot about W.R. Hotchkiss, who himself was an entrepreneur and small-business owner. Today I have the privilege to be the president and CEO of Deluxe, the company he founded in 1915. Mr. Hotchkiss created many new products and tried to start numerous businesses until he landed on a product that worked—the checkbook.

He took a $300 small-business loan and went door-to-door with his invention, selling the checkbook to businesses, banks—anyone who needed this new payment system—the same thing other small-business owners have done over the years with their inventions and ideas.

Mr. Hotchkiss took his product to the masses and, in doing so, found an audience and created the original payments company. From there, he improved the check and the checkbook, created other business forms, and built a company that was innovative and responsive. He did what any small-business owner would do: he learned and developed and grew his skills and his business.

Now to be clear, this book isn't about becoming the next Elon Musk or the next W.R. Hotchkiss. This book is about being a better small-businessperson, about taking what we have learned at Deluxe after more than 100 years serving small businesses and putting it together into tools, techniques, and tips to help businesses grow and thrive. It is about helping you learn and develop and grow your businesses, too.

Believe me, I know being a small-business owner is no small task. It takes a Herculean effort just to keep the doors open each day. And I mean it when I use that word: small-business owners are *heroes*. You employ millions of people. You keep commerce moving in your small town, community, or large city. You innovate and create. You inspire. Being a small-business owner is heroic, and our communities—locally and nationally—depend on you.

I believe strongly in how businesses, no matter the size, impact their communities. One of the things we talk about a lot at Deluxe is that we champion businesses so their communities can thrive. When people ask me what that means, I tell them our goal—and frankly it should be everyone's goal—is that businesses, no matter where they are located, have the help and resources they need to thrive so their communities can thrive.

The best way I can explain it is through an example from the reality TV show Deluxe produces called *Small Business Revolution*. Throughout this book, I share examples not only from the many customers we have helped in the past 100-plus years, but from the first five years of the series itself. Our concept is simple: we pick one small town or community to receive a $500,000 makeover from Deluxe, and we help six businesses and the community with business advice and physical makeovers.

In the first year in Wabash, Indiana, as we worked with the town, one business owner shared with us that he didn't see the point of what we were doing. He said the only businesses benefiting were those featured on the show. Yet a few weeks after his comments, his landscape business was hired by the city to build a new park on an empty lot downtown. Our team, in working with the community of Wabash, asked what needs the town had for aesthetic improvement. One was to improve this one corner where a burned building used to stand. So, Deluxe provided the funds, helped create the look, and then hired this small-business owner to bring the vision to life.

This small-business owner was able to build this beautiful park and pay his workers and himself, who in turn invested those dollars in other small businesses, and the cycle continued. He changed his tune when he saw that every dollar that goes into a small business—no matter where it comes from—in turn, cycles through the community in so many different ways. The small-business ecosystem sustains itself with each new dollar that comes in. Only when business succeeds are there funds for roads, schools, parks, health care, and more. In this way business is the core of a community's success.

That's why this book exists. After more than 100 years helping small businesses, we have learned a few things that can help your business, that can keep you on track or get you thinking differently about your next steps. In the following pages, I hope you'll find the advice, knowledge, and encouragement to follow in Mr. Hotchkiss's footsteps. Because when you do, it's not just you who benefits—our communities and country do too.

1

The Small Business: You Are a Very Big Part of America

You've Just Picked up this book and you're wondering if it's worth reading. The way I figure it, I have roughly 60 seconds before you decide, one way or the other. So, allow me to make that task unusually easy for you.

If you're a small-business owner, you are most likely working yourself to exhaustion on most days (and weekends). You have basically no time for your family, and you feel bad about that. But you're trying to support your family and community through your business.

The problem is that you've plowed your savings into your business and also may be close to maxing out your credit cards. You may not even be paying yourself a salary at this point, because you put yourself last in line. You care so very deeply about your employees and others who look to you to make this business carry on.

And you have secret doubts. *How can I work any harder? What can I do differently? Would somebody who knows about small-business success please give me some advice that I can believe in, advice that can help me? Or should I maybe throw in the towel at this point?*

If this does not sound like your situation, then maybe you don't need to read this book. But if my description sounds anything like the situation you're in, then this book may very well be the thing that changes the direction of your business.

We're in Your Corner

You may put on a strong and confident face to your family and employees, but I know the challenges you're facing as a small-business owner. I've started and run two successful small businesses, one when I was 15 years old painting houses and another in my thirties in the Silicon Valley around electronic payments. While I don't own a small business anymore, I run a big one. I'm the President and CEO of Deluxe, a Trusted Payments and Business Technology™ company that has been around for more than a century helping businesses succeed. Nearly 6,000 employees and their families look to me and my team for their livelihood, and millions of investors have trusted that their savings will grow by investing in our stock.

Your great-great-grandparents and every generation since has purchased checks from us, because we've been around since 1915. In fact, the founder of this company, W.R. Hotchkiss, invented the checkbook, making Deluxe the original payment company.

I wrote this book because Deluxe has an extremely unusual vantage point into the workings of small businesses. It's true, we provide services to literally thousands of some of the largest businesses on the planet. But we have more than four million customers, and millions of them are small businesses. They call us every day, not just to order more checks, but also to find out how we can help to grow their businesses. In fact, you might say that small businesses are our bread and butter.

We've evolved from being a check printer into providing many of the services that small businesses need to survive and thrive. Here's a short list of some of the services we offer to small businesses:

- Incorporation and business licensing services
- Checks and forms
- Logo design
- Trademark filing
- Designing, building, and hosting your website

- Marketing—both online and in print
- Promotional products
- Retail packaging
- Payroll solutions
- Online payments
- Merchant services (credit card acceptance and processing)

The list goes on. But here's what I want you to understand right from the start: **this is NOT a book about promoting Deluxe products and services,** like some long sales pitch. We have a great set of products and services, and you should check them out. There, that's my pitch.

But the truth is, you have bigger fish to fry at the moment. You're trying to keep your business afloat and the many other challenges that small businesses face.

This book is about how small businesses can successfully navigate big challenges.

If I'm able to help you through those challenges, I figure that you'll have gotten your money's worth from this book, and then some.

Seismic Events

On one level, we're still recovering from something of epic proportions with COVID. The world has had cases of deadly influenza before, in addition to plagues and such. Even so, the speed with which the coronavirus spread across the world has no precedent, with never-before-seen impact on small business.

So without any warning, you may have been having your best year ever, and the next month was your worst month ever. With no end in sight. Now your business may be recovering well, or still struggling for survival.

I don't need to recount all the COVID upheavals and lessons, but I want to point something out: if the only challenges small businesses faced were COVID or macroeconomic events, there might not be a need for this book. But there are so many other major challenges—which I call seismic events—that you also have to contend with. How many of these have happened to you?

- One or more big-box stores moved into town, and they slashed prices. In some cases, they can sell a product for less than you pay for the same product, wholesale.
- Amazon now sells just about everything, and there too it's almost impossible to match some of the prices. You know that in some cases your product is superior to the no-name item someone may buy on Amazon, but it's hard for customers to know the difference.
- When Washington, DC gets into a trade war with some country, the prices of raw materials can skyrocket. You sometimes see those roller-coaster prices in what you must buy.
- On a local level, one or more major employers downsized big time, or closed altogether, sending shockwaves throughout the community.
- Whether you have a 100 percent online business or yours is in a physical storefront, you're up against a bunch of competitors who are undercutting your prices or otherwise taking market share.

It's never been easy to start and run a business, but just one of these seismic events can put you out of business, never mind being in a situation where you're dealing with more than one.

I've written this book with these factors in mind. We're going to discuss several ways to counteract these pressures.

The *Small Business Revolution*

Deluxe has been a household name for generations, and we have been working with small businesses since day one back in 1915. Even so, you may not have heard about the *Small Business Revolution*.

It started as a marketing project to showcase the power of small businesses in our economy. To celebrate our 100th anniversary, we told the stories of 100 small businesses from across the country some years ago. It's kind of amazing that Deluxe has been around and helping businesses for almost half of America's history. Deluxe hired a brilliant marketer and brand expert, Amanda Brinkman, to create and guide that project. The result is an award-winning, beautifully produced video/television program viewed annually by millions of small business owners like you.

Long story short, we got a great response from the business community about the business lessons presented in a captivating and entertaining format.

You can watch the multiyear series from our website at deluxe.com/sbr and also on Hulu and Amazon Prime Video. If you haven't seen the series, you're in for a treat, if I do say so myself. You get a practical business education with real-world solutions to very real problems faced by a variety of businesses. You also get the benefit of the insights of the series host, our own Amanda Brinkman, and many of the experts she draws upon when constructing solutions for each business.

Not many people know this, but one of the factors that persuaded me to become CEO of Deluxe was my watching some seasons of *Small Business Revolution*, also known as *SBR*. I thought that if a corporation could share its 100-plus-year knowledge about business success, then it's a special place full of potential. I knew I wanted to be a part of that team, and I continue to be humbled to lead the Deluxe team and family.

I'm also humble enough to know that I don't personally have all the answers. So even though my name may be on the cover of this book, you should focus on the Deluxe name as the real source of the insights you will find on these pages. I think I'm reasonably good at certain aspects of business, and, as noted earlier, I built two small businesses myself years ago. The collective knowledge presented here draws from the experience of a whole team of specialists working together.

Leader to Leader

I do have another reason for writing this book, and it's to have a discussion with you, one-on-one, as much as can be done in a book.

There's a saying in our Deluxe company culture: "It's not about you." It's meant to make people with overly big egos stop and realize that they're not the center of the universe and accept the reality that they are part of something much bigger than themselves. That's certainly a message some people need to hear. However, senior leaders on our team have heard me say the opposite, and for a very good reason. I'll say: "It's all about you."

I don't mean that statement in the egotistical sense, but in the sense that you must step up and be leaders. As a business owner, it really is all about you. When you decide to hire people and therefore build an organization, everyone is looking to you as the owner of the business to chart a course. You need to be inspirational at times and tough at times. People look to you not just to be managed, but to be led.

I can speak from experience that it's very difficult to do. As the business owner, you get to see all the inadequacies of your situation at one time: you need to pay bills, fill open positions, compete with the new shop down the block, and bring in next month's revenues to make payroll.

You need to set prices that are low enough to not drive away your customers, but high enough to keep the doors open. You need to keep an eye on the competition and somehow find a way to keep your customers coming back.

And after long, fitful nights with all these pressures weighing on you, somehow you need to keep your team thinking and acting positively, when that is the *last thing* you're feeling. Does this ring a bell?

I, too, answered the calling to start and run a small business. I started a painting company in the middle of a recession, because there were no jobs for unskilled young people. Later, I was working in a well-paying safe corporate job at the time, but the urge to build something of my own was just too strong. I took the leap.

And a big leap it was. Talk about an emotional roller-coaster. Over the course of a relatively short period, I felt elation and despair. I was proud at times and at the end of my rope too many times to count. You know what I'm talking about, so I don't have to explain this to you, other than to say that it really can be the best feeling and the worst. And sometimes those feelings can happen on the same day, right?

I sold that business and didn't find another opportunity that I felt strongly enough to create another business around. These days I'm trying to make a difference in a big company. I certainly don't have all the answers, and I have my share of nights with not much sleep leading our global team. But I've learned a few things in my long career, and I will share them with you in this book.

One thing I've discovered: no matter how small your business is, or how large, there are certain surprising similarities. In other words, when you're starting out, you may think that if you eventually become a million-dollar business, or a Fortune 500 business, that you'll have arrived and your major problems will be solved. You'll be on the business equivalent of Easy Street.

That's when I think about Walter Annenberg, a businessman who was so wealthy he gave away more than $2 billion in his lifetime.[1] Here's what he had to say about success:

> I want to remind you that success in life is based on hard slogging. There will be periods when discouragement is great and upsetting, and the antidote for this is calmness and fortitude and a modest yet firm belief in your competence. Be sure that your priorities are in order so that you can proceed in a logical manner and be ever mindful that nothing will take the place of persistence.

As leaders of businesses large or small, we can meet our challenges by applying hard-learned lessons from others to help us succeed. In this book we're sharing 100 years of our own hard-learned lessons, so you don't have to endure the same pain.

You May Be Thinking This

I'm not surprised that the businesses chosen by Deluxe on SBR did well. If I had Deluxe appear at my door and pay for stuff plus bring a huge team to work with me, I could improve a lot, too.

It may be true that you'd improve much if you were featured on SBR, but that's not the point. Even when we select a small town or neighborhood in a big city, only a handful of businesses get the chance to work directly with us. I agree that it's pretty cool for a business to get chosen, but the coolness does not stop with them.

This book will give you far more than what is in the television series, in two very important ways. We're limited in terms of what we can pack into episodes. Television does not lend itself to an in-depth treatment of a dozen or so aspects of each business—but this book will do that for you. The book also summarizes common themes and provides integrated advice about common business challenges supported by multiple examples.

In addition, you do not have to go through an application and interview process, with long odds that your business will be chosen.

In reality, we receive nominations from thousands of towns each year, and in each of those towns, there are hundreds of eligible small businesses. In the end, millions of votes are cast to help us choose the area to highlight for a new season. Being one of the handful chosen for *SBR* is like winning the lottery.

This book stacks the odds in your favor, because you're holding the playbook for recognizing certain situations, and you have an easy reference guide detailing the best practices for handling those situations.

In a way, you're in the same situation as even those lucky businesses were, when we were done filming and had to go home. The most fundamental success factor of all is in taking regular and effective action toward a worthy goal. Our personalized boost is certainly a big help to those businesses, but is by no means enough to create long-lasting success. That can only come from the many regular actions that they must take, and that you must also take. By the end of this book, you'll know exactly what steps you must follow to create that long-term success.

Companion Site

I have more good news for you. We have developed a companion website to this book. Some best practices in business are timeless, like certain effective leadership techniques. Other best practices are highly dynamic, like the best ways to be found by search engines.

In this book we give you a wide variety of these techniques. As those practices change, or we identify additional ones, we'll update the companion site accordingly. You can find it at deluxe.com/SBRbook.

You Are Part of a Worthy Tradition

I'm a huge believer that small businesses are the bedrock foundation of our communities, and also of our country. In any large or small city in America, the number of small businesses is much greater than the number of big employers. Small businesses create the majority of new jobs in our country and provide essential services to fellow citizens on a local and national level. Clearly, I don't want to take anything away from the big employers, because we are one of them! Large companies were once small companies too, and they also have a key role in community success, employing hundreds or even many thousands of people.

However, it's the small businesses that make up Main Street, before the big employers come to town and after they leave. It's where all the services are created that a community needs: auto repair, hair salon, watering hole, pizza parlor, health service, literacy center, and dozens of others. And it's where a huge variety of jobs are formed, money changes hands, and taxes get paid to pave the streets, build schools and parks, and deliver health care. In fact, big businesses don't move into towns unless the small businesses have already provided the solid foundation of people and services to make it all work.

This Guide Can Also Help You to Start a Business

One of the Deluxe companies is MyCorp, which offers cloud-based incorporation services for people who want to start businesses. That company gives us a unique window into the state of business formation in the United States. It was remarkable to see: in the midst of the coronavirus pandemic, the number of businesses formed skyrocketed. According to our data from MyCorp, business incorporations were up 11 percent year-over-year during the pandemic.

Clearly this pandemic caused people to stop and think about the jobs they had, or lost, and what other options there were. In some cases, they decided that this was the time to make their business dreams come true.

If you're one of those people, and you picked up this book in the hope that it might give you a boost to your brand-new business, you're absolutely right.

Our Deluxe team found in producing SBR virtually every business either was not using certain powerful business practices at all or they were using them ineffectively. For example, many businesses had no website, or their site was ancient and by no means presented the operation in the best light. In some cases, their site was solid, but the business was not using some other business-building method effectively, like email marketing.

In a sense, new businesses can especially benefit from this book, because they don't need to unplug or unlearn outdated practices. They can start fresh and in the direction that's been proven to work, instead of having to figure it all out the hard way.

How *SBR* Analyzed Businesses, and How This Book Is Organized

You can see from the Contents that most of the chapters are on specific business-growth principles. Certainly, it's possible to dip in and out, depending on what you need at the moment. However, you'll benefit the most from reading this book in the order that you find the chapters.

In the *SBR* series, we followed a methodical approach to helping businesses. First, we got acquainted (as we have in this first chapter). Then we sat down with the business owners and got a sense of how the business came about, and what the revenue and expense situation look like. Then we explored the assets of the business, not so much in terms of equipment but the products and services that are most successful.

Then the discussion shifted to the positioning of the business in the community: where business comes from, what we know about customers, and what the unique positioning of the business is, if any. There's also a discussion of the competition or any other seismic events facing the business.

The final part of the interview revolved around some difficult discussions and initial actions to be taken. In some cases that meant bringing in special talent to the business or making sure that written agreements existed among friends. Business has a way of testing friendships; if you have a real business, you might start with a handshake, but you need to follow up with something in writing.

In the *SBR* series, this is the point at which the Deluxe team of experienced professionals like Amanda, Julie Gordon, Cameron Potts, and many others rolled up their sleeves and brought their expertise to bear. Each episode is a bit different, but also similar in certain respects.

That's where this book will be particularly handy to you. The chapters do a deep dive into key business elements, and especially where many small businesses run into trouble. As you read each chapter, either make notes in the margins or have some paper handy, because you'll need it. This is a read-think-and-do kind of book, and not some new business theory that doesn't get specific.

You're likely to find one chapter may be pretty familiar information to you, and several others are not. This also will vary by business, but I can tell you this: we chose some great businesses in the many episodes of *SBR*, and not a single one of them was successfully using all the advice that we cover in these chapters.

Now that I've given you some perspective on what this book is about and how it can help you, it's time to ask some hard questions about your business. That's the topic of Chapter 2.

2

Why? Tough Questions, Tough Decisions

I Frequently Speak with small-business owners around the country. Sometimes we have the chance to sit down over coffee or a meal—or, more recently, over Zoom. I have certain questions that I've found to be most useful in understanding their businesses. Perhaps the most important question: "Why are you doing what you're doing?"

With some of the businesses we see in the *SBR* series, the answer may be: "I love to bake." In the case of Ohm Nohm Bakery & Cafe in Season 5, Episode 5, we met the owner, Jessamine Daly-Griffen. She was a devoted mother of kids who needed gluten-free baked goods. For her, the original "why" was "I couldn't find healthy and delicious baked goods for my family nearby, so I decided to make them myself." That's a wonderful example of taking matters into your own hands and solving a problem. I tip my hat to her.

Here's the interesting thing: your "why" may change over time, and that's okay.

However, I cannot overstate the importance of being clear with yourself about why you are starting or have started a business.

While your "why" may adapt at different times, *what cannot change is the ability of the business to create sufficient income to support its owners and workers. That is the point of a business. If it can't support the owner and workers, it probably isn't a business at all.*

When we look at Jessamine's gluten-free business, she could have just continued to bake those items at home for her family. Instead, she got into business. Why? Because word spread about her excellent baked goods that solved a serious health need and were not available anywhere else in the counties surrounding Fredonia, New York. She ramped up her operation into a commercial enterprise to meet that important need for other families.

Many businesses start as a noble pursuit, to do something nice for neighbors or the community, and many owners dream about the business being able to comfortably support their families at the same time. Many groups can organize themselves like a business. Nonprofits are a great example of organizations that are organized similarly to businesses.

Every business needs to provide a source of income for the owner and team of workers helping the business succeed. Just because you want something to be a profitable business does not mean it has that potential.

Perhaps the business can be successful, but not in your location. Or perhaps the business is already successful in the current location, but it's potential for more is limited by some factor. Maybe the business is better as a hobby than a business, or maybe a hobby has the potential to become a great business.

When a Hobby Becomes a Business

Some people's businesses begin as hobbies. They let off steam (or save money) by building furniture, and then people take notice and ask to have something built. Other people have hobbies that stay hobbies, and that's cool too. In the case of Jessamine, it was not a hobby but a critical need for her family to have gluten-free food. But Jessamine can't work for free, simply to provide her neighbors gluten-free food. She needs to provide for her family and have a reasonable return on the investment of her time, talent, and treasure.

So when does a fun, helpful, or important activity become a business? There are several markers for when that occurs. It starts to become a business when you:

- Invest in commercial equipment to make things faster
- Sign a lease
- Quit your day job
- Hire employees
- Begin to take substantial sums from your savings, or you pay for the activity on your personal credit cards, or both

Somewhere along the line, when you've passed enough of these markers, you're a business. Becoming a small business is a very big deal. Now you have other people and their families depending on you for their very livelihood. You may be taking on liability if someone slips and falls in your establishment, or if a product you sent from your online business gets misused in some way.

It's at this point of becoming a business that people need to ask once again: "Why am I doing what I'm doing?," but the fact is most people don't ask it again. As far as I can tell, most of the SBR businesses did not ask this critical question. They started the activity, and their "why" at the time might have been clear. Then they gradually morphed into a business, but nobody told them to ask that key question once more.

A business needs to have a purpose, and the purpose can be anything you want it to be. It can be that you're going to run a nonprofit bakery, or that your town needs a combination golf course and community center that will be run partially through donations.

The problem happens when someone is running a store or other organization that's become a business and they reach their breaking point. They get to the place where they are often overwhelmed and not making enough money to pay themselves. They're running today's larger business with the "why" or purpose that they started with five years ago, when it was just a hobby.

For the vast majority of businesses we've worked with over the years and most recently showcased in SBR, their current purpose doesn't typically involve making a fortune and becoming a national sensation; however, it does involve making a living, which certainly is a reasonable and necessary goal.

When It's Right to Be Brutal

When you ask the tough question of why you want to be in business, and if you decide that you do want to make a reasonable profit from it, then you need to ask yourself three other questions:

1. Is there truly a market for what I'm doing?
2. If there is a market, can I deliver the products or services profitably?
3. If so, how long will it take me to get to that profitability from where I am today?

Those are tough questions! Here you're already operating a business; am I really suggesting that you need to step back and ask these fundamental questions at the same time? *Yes.* You'll have the best chance of meeting your goal of making a living from your business if you have a brutally honest review at this stage.

In the case of Ellen's Bridal & Dress Boutique in Season 1, Episode 3, owner Lisa Downs was able to get a handle on the size of her potential market by finding out how many marriage licenses were issued in Wabash County each year.

When it comes to the second question of profitability, this is where you need to know your numbers, even if some of them were from your hobby days. If you've been making a profit at times, that's great. What have been your most profitable products or services? What were the least profitable? As we discuss in Chapter 3 about crucial numbers to know, do you have a handle on the maximum profitability of your operation as it exists today?

That third question requires a tough assessment: What are the numbers telling you, and are they moving in the direction of crossing over into regular profitability?

It's not the end of the world if they're not showing profitability—*if* you are willing to make changes.

Course Corrections

Don't get me wrong: I'm the last person to want to put a damper on people starting businesses. Those brave people are a major target market for Deluxe. But what I am suggesting is that running a business is a bit like flying a plane. If you ever look at the route that commercial pilots take when crossing the country, you will see that it is never a straight line from takeoff to landing. They're continually making course adjustments as instructed by air traffic controllers, in order to avoid other planes and skirt around bad weather.

As a business owner, you also need to get your bearings on a regular basis and analyze where you are, where you're going, and what it will take to get there. In the *SBR* series, we saw many times where the current course would not allow the owners—no matter how hard they worked—to make ends meet and keep the doors open, never mind pay themselves a modest sum.

Therefore, to reach the destination of staying open and paying themselves, often the *SBR* businesses would have to raise prices or think of ways to trim inventory, menu items, or services offered, and other creative solutions.

Much of this book is a guide to helping you through the process of asking important questions and giving you options: it's thinking about these questions that allows you to get your bearings as a business. They involve where you are financially, what your products and services are, and how you stack up to your competition, among many other considerations.

In the course of filming many seasons of *SBR*, the Deluxe team has conducted literally hundreds of interviews with small businesses, and our team talks to millions of small businesses every month. We have never come across a business where the owner said: "I started the business because I was a business-school graduate and I wanted to put into practice the ideas I learned in the classroom."

We think business schools are great and they can teach many valuable skills. I had the good fortune to graduate from one of the country's top business schools—Northwestern University's Kellogg Graduate School of Management. I am profoundly grateful for the privilege to learn at Kellogg, and for all the tools added to my kit. But having a world-class toolkit alone did not inspire me to start a business. People start businesses about something they care about, something where they can answer "why."

The "why" almost universally is, at least in large part, about earning a living.

Behind the scenes at *SBR*: we met Jonas Janek in Season 3. Jonas and his business didn't make it on to the show, but he left a lasting impression as a small business owner who thought through these questions. Jonas and his wife, Andrea, live in Alton, Illinois, a bedroom community of St. Louis. They both enjoyed productive careers in big business for many years, but Jonas wanted to do his own thing. He wanted to open a business to do custom, high-end metal fabrication for any number of projects in the area.

A business executive, Jonas asked all the right questions. Yes, there was a market for what he wanted to do in a large urban area. Could he deliver products and services profitably? Yes, indeed he could. And how long before profitability? He worked all that out as well. Jonas was methodical and exacting. He bought the equipment he needed and hired skilled workers. Even through the pandemic, Jensen Fabrication thrived, and a lot of that had to do with the right questions Jonas asked and answered.

We have many medium and large businesses as customers of Deluxe. In fact, if you just focus on financial institutions, we have more than 4,000 of them as customers. Many small businesses are customers of our financial institution customers. This makes our customers' customer our customer too. That's why *we love small businesses*—it's where the proverbial rubber meets the road in America.

As a small-business owner, you are continually faced with the challenge of navigating the unknown:

- Can I afford to hire another person?
- How do I get more customers in the door without spending a ton of money (which I don't have) on advertising?
- How can I possibly compete with the mega corporations that have moved into my territory?
- And many more.

Your ability to pivot when new circumstances present themselves is as crucial as whatever skill you bring to the table with the products and services you offer.

Seeing the World as It Really Is

I come from a very long line of proud teachers. That's been the occupation of my mom, sister, mother-in-law, brother-in-law, several aunts, cousins, a niece and nephew, and an uncle too. I've met some of their students and I can confidently say that these and other teachers genuinely change lives for the better. Who's more noble than a math teacher who also is the basketball coach, and who takes a deep interest in teaching kids not just about school subjects or sports, but about life? The same is true for the drama teacher bringing students together to produce a show, or the music teacher producing a concert. In some cases, a teacher might be the only really positive role model in a kid's life. Teachers change lives.

Here's where seeing the world as it really is comes in: if you decide to be that teacher, then the job comes with certain realities—you may have quite a few weeks off in the summer, but you won't get rich. You can have this amazing impact on young people's lives, but don't get mad that you can't afford Paris every summer and can't have a Ferrari in the driveway, because that's not the reality of being a teacher. Teachers should be paid far more than they are, but unfortunately they aren't. If you choose that line of work, then make peace with its realities.

It's the same in business. Every business started as a small business. I started my career at Procter & Gamble. P&G was started by two guys who needed to make a living and decided to make soap and candles. P&G was founded 184 years ago and is now a global giant with more than $70 billion in revenue in 2020. Deluxe started similarly with a guy needing to provide for his family, and he invented the checkbook 106 years ago.

Not every business will turn into a P&G or Deluxe. In fact, the vast majority will stay small businesses, and sadly most will fail within five years.

You can make a fortune in business, of course, but so much depends on what you sell, where you sell it, and to whom. Not all business ideas, locations, and opportunities are the same. And that is more than okay. But as a business owner, it is essential you understand the realistic potential of your business and make peace with the opportunity at hand.

If you have a local product like a restaurant, then your maximum potential customer base is defined by driving distance from your restaurant. Similarly, if you sell a low-cost product, you may have a few buyers but you may *need* hundreds of buyers just to break even.

Our choices determine the trade-offs we must live with. Therefore, see your business potential as it really is, and not how you wish it to be; then decide if that's acceptable to you. Then make peace with your decision and get to work.

Here's the good news: you can think accurately and realistically about any business, and still find ways to grow most substantially. That's what this book is largely about. You just need to do it with your eyes open, and with as little wishful thinking as possible.

Four Crucial Decisions

If there's one thing that distinguishes small-business owners from lots of other people, it's how they must make tons of decisions without having the large staff and fancy reports that the big businesses can rely upon for support.

Let's talk about four of those many decisions—four that you *always make*, whether you realize it or not. How you decide will largely determine how successful you are in business. That's a bold statement, but it's based on our experience with businesses. So here goes:

Decision 1: Change Nothing or Decide to Change Something

This is the most fundamental decision for you to answer. On a daily basis we all have this decision to make about our business. Sometimes it's about mundane things like the front door to your store driving you crazy by slamming shut 100 times a day. However, it's not bad enough to do anything about it until something triggers you. It might be a customer within earshot, talking to another customer about how she so hates to be in your store for more than five minutes because of that door.

You live with something, or you decide to change it. Of course, the same is true about vitally important issues like "Will I raise my prices?" or "Should I give Bob one last chance about keeping the food temperatures in compliance so we're not shut down by the health department?"

You can continue on the course you're on, and probably get the results you've gotten. If your business is doing well, then more power to you. However, I suspect that you're reading this book because you want to find a way out of the hamster wheel that is draining all of your time and resources, and you're looking for a solution. If that is the case, then you've taken action by reading this book, and that's great. But the larger action you'll have to take is on the options and recommendations we give you in the book.

Decision 2: Make All the Mistakes Yourself or Learn from Others

There's a certain semi-positive aura around working your way up from beginner to expert and having all the scars to show for it. "Hard-earned experience" and "hard-earned money" have kind of an honest feel to them.

You need to get out of that mindset and learn as much as you can from others. One of my favorite quotes is from German Chancellor Otto von Bismarck, roughly a century ago, who said: "Fools say 'experience is the best teacher.' I prefer to learn from other people's experience."

The last time you went to the bank to make a deposit, I trust that the teller did not say: "Did you earn this money from a painful process of trial and error? You did? Well then, we'll double your deposit."

Kids learn from falling down and getting up, and we do them no favors by being helicopter parents, always shielding them from whatever. But this book is about your business and how to be resilient in the face of numerous challenges and setbacks. When you're in business, the expense clock is forever ticking, and time is simply too short to make all of the mistakes yourself.

Major Success Tip. Here's where many people get hung up. *They think: Hey, I'm willing to learn from others, but the problem is that my business is unique. Those other businesses are not exactly like mine, even when they're in the same industry. I have to find out for myself.*

Well, yes and no. Yes, there is no other music studio at 123 Main Street where yours is, so in that sense you're unique. But that does not make 90 percent (or is it 98 percent?) of your challenges any different from what other businesses face. The fact that at some cosmic level you are unique is fine; but how you should post images on Instagram is no different, and how you make your website look appealing should follow certain tested and proven principles.

What successful businesspeople do is look for similarities, not differences. If you're watching the episode in Season 3 about Lovett's, which is famous for selling the best fried pig snoots around, you may conclude that your law practice has nothing to learn from that episode.

The better way to approach it is to be taking notes when the Deluxe team noted that Lovett's had not used all its "designators" or tags that Google allows businesses to be known by. For example, "restaurant" may be a tag, but Lovett's didn't think to add "soul food" as a tag, and that turned out to make a big difference in more people discovering Lovett's.

The takeaway for an attorney should be: I wonder what tag Google has us under? Probably "law firm" but maybe there is an additional one for "personal injury attorney," "estate planning services," or "real estate law."

Ignore all the differences and focus on what you can extract of value from any business you come across. A soul-food restaurant might get an idea from a dog-grooming operation that has an open floor plan where you can see the dogs being groomed. Maybe people would enjoy seeing all those snoots being smoked (maybe not); it's worth thinking about.

Decision 3: Follow the Recipe, or Strike Out on Your Own

I'm a firm believer in following instructions or recipes as closely as possible at first. Then later on, experiment to your heart's content. Unfortunately, many people will see a set of instructions and kind-of, sort-of follow them while adding their own twist. Then if the desired outcome doesn't happen, they blame the instructions.

The way I see it, you want the help of someone who's been down a particular road before. You may not understand why the instructions are the way they are, but if you've found an expert, trust the expert. Then after you've followed those instructions as closely as you can, evaluate the results. If possible, discuss it with the expert. Only then is it the time to modify anything. As with the other decisions, this is something you make, one way or another, whether you're conscious of it or not.

In Season 4, Casey Cox wanted help to expand or franchise her successful Nooma Life yoga studios. She opened Nooma in Searcy, Arkansas, to an incredible response and subsequently opened two more locations in Arkansas. Casey was sitting on a great brand, packed studios, and a potential franchise concept, but she was spending time on the wrong things. She loved to choreograph the sessions and create new routines, but that wasn't where the money was.

We brought in Stacey Anderson, president of Anytime Fitness, to help Casey focus on what would bring her more value. Stacey helped Casey think beyond the routines to membership prices, social media, paying herself, and empowering her employees. It was the kind of "been there, done that" recipe/help that gave Casey the confidence she needed. Though her passion lay in creating and teaching her classes, success would come from focusing on the business elements.

Decision 4: Bag It Early, or Push on Through

Success does not follow a straight line. Running a business involves many different skills, and those take time to develop. For example, with many of the businesses we highlighted in the *SBR* series, they were not using social media effectively. Some didn't use it at all, and others would post a few things but not in a way that generated maximum visibility for the brand and company.

The reality of social media is that it does not require one massive effort, but instead the steady creation and publishing of posts and images over time. The social-media platforms like Facebook, Instagram, Pinterest, LinkedIn, and others have highly sophisticated algorithms that closely monitor who is a regular contributor and who only posts stuff once in a while. They don't give much visibility to those who occasionally post, and they reward the regular contributors with visibility.

Now imagine a tired, busy, "broke" business owner who decides to try social media because she heard it might work. The owner creates a few posts and—not much happens. She tries again with a few posts, and maybe gets even fewer views or comments.

This is a crucial moment for the business owner. Does she keep going with her social-media efforts, or bag it and try something else? She'll make the decision, one way or another.

Unfortunately, if she is not able to ask a social-media expert about what to do, she's likely to call it quits. "Hey, I tried. I guess this social-media stuff doesn't work in my case." Most likely an expert would have had suggestions on how to improve posts, but the real benefit of the expert would be to say, "You've got to give this some time! Rome wasn't built in a day and a social-media presence takes weeks and even months to really catch on." An expert will also be able to know when an effort has in fact gone on long enough and should be modified or stopped.

Some business owners sprint for 200 yards and are looking around for a medal when business growth is more like a marathon, and they have another 26 miles to go.

Be Like a Duck

Sometimes simple imagery is best. I am known for saying that if you're in business, you need to be like a duck. You might have a difficult conversation with a customer, employee, or business partner, and it can get you down pretty quickly. That's when I think about three traits of a duck:

First, they're super buoyant. They may land on the water and go under, but invariably they'll bob right back to the surface.

Second, they're water repellant. No matter how much of a drenching they get, they tuck their wings tight, give themselves a quick shake and the water simply runs off their back.

Finally, no matter how hard they're paddling underwater, they present the same pleasant demeanor to anyone who's looking.

I've learned that as a business owner, you just don't have the luxury of letting things get to you for long. There's no time in business for a "bad day." If you bake cakes and are having a bad day, you might ruin someone's wedding cake. Not only will your bad day have ruined someone's wedding, you'll have ruined your reputation too.

Of course, you feel setbacks and put-downs. You're human. But what counts is how quickly you recover and move on. *Be like a duck. Tuck your wings, shake it off, and pedal onward.*

Work-Life Integration

Not long ago I was invited to speak to a community leadership class. It was associated with a social service agency and they were working hard to grow a group of community leaders who could then go out and be involved in nonprofit organizations like themselves. I could tell that the audience was filled with very motivated achievers in their 30s and 40s.

One of the questions I got was: "I have a young family with kids. How can I get all this done and possibly achieve work/life balance?"

I told the group that was the wrong paradigm. If you think of a balance beam or a kids' teeter-totter, almost all of the time one end is higher than the other. So, if we put work on one side and life on the other, how can you possibly achieve any significant height on one side without sacrificing the other side? It's the wrong imagery, the wrong paradigm. Successful businesspeople don't see work and life as two separate and competing activities.

I'm not a gambling man, but I think a closer analogy to something physical is a deck of cards. Let's say that your work life consists of being dealt 15 cards, and your home life consists of another 15 cards that you're dealt. That's 30 cards. There are another 22 cards in that deck, and you can use them to balance out those hands. The extra 22 cards are how you use your time, and how creative you are. It is not a "zero-sum" game where one extra card on the work side means taking a card away from the life side.

As CEO of Deluxe, I have a significant number of obligations to the company outside of regular business hours. I could tell my wife that "duty calls" and as a former divisional chief financial officer at General Electric in their glory days and a KPMG alum, she would fully understand the drill. Long ago, we decided to be far more creative and look at those obligations instead as opportunities for us to be together doing something interesting. We'll go to dinner before an event, or afterward we'll get a cocktail or dessert. In this way we are integrating our life, fulfilling meaningful obligations, and still enjoy being together. This is much better than pouting that we had lost our Saturday night.

Similarly, we often entertain business colleagues and customers in our home. During the pandemic, Deluxe broadcast our annual customer event, the Deluxe Exchange, from a studio close to our home. In the middle of the day, I asked my wife if we should invite the marketing team over for a casual dinner that same evening. She agreed and our whole family sprang into action. We arranged and served dinner for 15 guests a few hours later, and our kids were part of the evening too. The kids set the table, Jean Ann prepped the meal, and I ran the grill. That dinner wasn't about choosing either work or family; it was an example of life integration, including our kids and a boyfriend and girlfriend of two of our kids too.

As a small-business owner, another brother-in-law and his wife do the same thing. They own two Ace Hardware stores in small towns in the Midwest. Keeping small businesses going in small towns is hard work, as we've plainly seen from *SBR*.

Anyway, they constantly must be creative in order to integrate work with the rest of their lives. The Ace Hardware tag line is "Ace Is the Place with the Helpful Hardware Folks." If one week they're short staffed in one of the stores, they don't have the luxury of simply hanging a sign on the door: "today we can't be the Helpful Hardware Folks." Instead, they hold off on the administrative activities like paying bills and ordering inventory so everyone can be on the floor, helping customers. That means sometimes they get takeout dinner on Sunday night and spend a few hours together in the office, catching up on the back-office work. Yes, they are working on a Sunday night. Yes, they are working extra hours. And yes, they are enjoying being together enjoying nice takeout.

Another brother-in-law founded a regional CPA practice in a Big 10 college town. He and his wife enjoy warm weather in the winter. They travel to Florida occasionally through the winter. He works there a few weeks at a time, getting to enjoy the sunshine, even in the middle of annual tax season.

One of my sisters and her husband are well-known folk musicians and recording artists. My sister also writes haiku poems and has published several volumes complete with beautiful self-shot photography. In addition to now being a full-time development director for a major zoo, she has turned her passion into a part-time small business where she sells her art online. Rather than building a studio somewhere else, she set up an area at in her basement where she can invest available pockets of time to write and record. She and her husband integrate their passion into their regular lives, rather than it being a scheduled, separate part of their lives.

Another sister is a trial lawyer who, along with other partners, left a large law firm to form a more nimble, complex litigation boutique firm. The move gave her greater flexibility, including the opportunity to take an international sabbatical in support of nonprofits. By choosing to live in the city she had easy access to amenities and avoided a long commute. She filled her need for the outdoors on weekends at state parks. All of this in combination created an integrated whole life, not an "either-or" life.

Life integration is about making choices, and simply deciding, not letting circumstances decide for you. Choosing to make a decision is very empowering, and very critical. *Any time you avoid making a decision, you have made a decision. Choose an integrated life.*

All of us have now experienced some of this integration, having survived COVID with kids at home from school, dogs barking on Zoom calls, and the unexpected kid walking through your WebEx interview. When you think about life integration, instead of the impossible teeter-totter, you really can find a happy balance of what is important to you.

Put Your Mask on First

There is one other decision you must make. As I've already mentioned, it's been very common for business owners we feature on *SBR* to not be taking a salary. That fact emerges after a painful discussion of the financials. But usually there's more pain to be seen in the episodes, in the form of a candid review of what options are open to the owner in order to be able to draw a salary from the business.

You can see their reluctance to charge more. It's like they're willing to continue to endure the long days and short bank balances. After all, many customers are friends, and they're often doing financially worse than the owner. The Deluxe team frequently needs to drive home the point that this "business flight" is airborne and about to run out of gas, due either to no funds, no life integration, ruined health, or some combination of these.

That's where the business owner needs to remember the safety briefing we've all heard a hundred times on airplanes. *You need to put your mask on first, before helping loved ones.* Why? To be selfish? No, it's so you'll be able to help others, not be slumped unconscious in your seat.

Your customers will understand if you need to put your mask on first and charge an extra dollar for that food item or service. A few won't get it, of course. But all of your customers will be worse off if the "Closed" sign on your front door one day never gets moved to "Open."

~~~

In the next chapter, we talk about critical numbers and financials.

3

Crucial Numbers

THERE IS A book that's well known to people who study success, called *Think and Grow Rich*, by Napoleon Hill. However, an even more interesting book is *The Laws of Success*, by the same author.[1] In it, Hill writes that one of the success laws is "accurate thought."

Thinking accurately sounds like a simple thing to do, but it's in fact extremely challenging. We humans are big bundles of emotions, hopes, dreams, and survival mechanisms. As a result, we all can recall times when we looked at someone else's irrational actions and wondered: *What could they have been thinking?*

Well, we're going to follow a process now that will allow us to look at your business with accurate thought. We'll assess how it's doing right now, rather than how we'd like it to be doing.

You may know from watching *SBR* episodes that pretty early in the process, the business owner will travel to our offices to meet some of our team of experts.

Amanda and other experts will have an early and critically important discussion around "the numbers," and it's usually pretty awkward. That's the typical emotion because almost without exception, the business owner does not have a good grasp of key financial information. In fact, in some cases the owner knows next to nothing about how their business is doing financially.

Back-Pocket Accounting

If you think about the common situation with respect to what small-business owners know about their numbers, you could call it "back-pocket accounting." They have their bank account statement and credit card statement with available credit in their left back pocket, and they have a pile of bills in their right back pocket.

In a good month, if the left pocket can cover all the bills due in the right pocket, the owner can breathe a sigh of only temporary relief. In a sense, this is not surprising, because there are very few businesses that were started where the owner was thinking, "I created this business because I have such a passion for accounting."

I want to say right up front that accounting is an honorable and absolutely vital profession. My brother-in-law runs an accounting firm in the Midwest for years. I'm married to a CPA too. The world would be chaos without someone keeping track of things, and we have many great accounting specialists at Deluxe. But even accountants have to admit that accounting can become quite complicated at times, and to do it properly requires training, skill, and experience.

Even for a small business, things like payroll accounting, state and federal filings, tax treatment of depreciable equipment, and other concepts can very quickly become overwhelming. Oh, and that's just being overwhelmed with accounting tasks, never mind all the other activities needed to run a business.

It's no wonder then that we humans, when confronted with financial complexities, may think we're streamlining and simplifying when we revert to back-pocket accounting. Plus, after all, as long as the cash is available from somewhere, it kind of seems to work. We might even know several other business owners who use the same "system."

The problem with this kind of financial management is that it's dangerous. When you live financially day to day without a more organized process, you can't see things coming.

In business it's common to say things like: "Let's examine this issue from the 30,000-foot level," meaning look at the big strategic picture. Then there's the tactical level of 5,000 feet or so, and the daily operations at ground level. Well, using that analogy, doing back-pocket accounting is like being a squirrel darting across a road at the one-inch level. You don't notice the car until two seconds before it's upon you, and if you jump soon enough, you might make it across—until you don't.

For example, more than 40 percent of businesses every year get run over by a tax penalty.[2] A great many of these situations are unforced errors, due to back-pocket accounting. Given how tight money is for many businesses, this kind of mistake could be catastrophic.

This type of accounting also does not give you options. You can't plan ahead or make course corrections because your numbers are not organized, even on the simplest of spreadsheets or written out somewhere.

In the first two seasons of *SBR* our co-host was celebrity, entrepreneur, and investor Robert Herjavec. At one point, Robert said that in his experience with small businesses, what leads to failure, "Across the board, it's the lack of financial knowledge about their businesses."

What you'll notice with the *SBR* episodes is that the businesses are not asked to get crazy-granular about their numbers. Yes, you need an accountant who can do all the filings and someone to do payroll and tax calculations. But you don't need highly detailed financial analysis for the business-growth project that we'll do together in this book.

One-Sheet Accounting

And yes, the back-pocket accounting approach has to stop, or at least it needs to be augmented with what I call one-sheet accounting. You need to up your game and your knowledge of where you stand financially, and you can do it on just one sheet of paper. It's the 80/20 Rule at work, where you can get a great deal of benefit from a handful of key numbers.

The important thing here is to not be spooked by accounting terms, and to not give up on this process. It may be something of a pain at first to gather this information. Just trust me and do it, okay?

Revenue

This is an important concept. With back-pocket accounting, you just focused on the cash on hand, or, even worse, the money you are borrowing. When getting a handle on our finances, what we first want to do is go upstream and look at the raw dollars that come in the door. That's your revenue.

This means knowing what people paid you, before you consider any expenses. Many businesses get their revenue from product sales. Some will get revenue from other things like membership or subscription fees paid, or they may own some real estate and they get paid rent or royalties. Other examples of revenue are interest paid on a bank account, commissions, and profits from the sale of something.

Accountants may go crazy at this point because instead they'll want to talk about "operating income" and "non-operating income." That's all cool and necessary for preparing documents to file with the government, but I'm going to resist getting into the technical weeds so we can keep our discussion focused on broad concepts.

In the back-pocket world you're not accustomed to thinking about revenues, and that's because you can't spend revenues. You can only spend cash flow. More on that in a minute.

Our focus now is to write down all the different, separate sources of money coming *in the door*, without paying attention yet to what makes it to your back pocket. Also, if you receive certain revenue not monthly but less frequently, write down how much you can expect from whom, and how frequently.

Expenses

You're no doubt painfully familiar with this number, because it's mostly all those bills bulging in your back pocket. They may be almost all of your expenses, but just make sure that you also write down any expenses that are not monthly. Business taxes are often overlooked. You might have some software services that charge you an annual fee, or you may subscribe to something that charges you quarterly.

Look through your bank statements or the big pile of paid bills that you stuck in a shoebox and write down anything that occurs less frequently than every month. While you're at it, note how often this expense happens, how much it is for, and when the next payment is due.

There's another critical factor with expenses, and that is to make a note of expenses you're obligated to pay contractually over time. For example, if you've signed a lease for three years, note both the amount you're paying and also that the lease is for three years. If you know that the numbers will change, make a note of that, too. Your lease payment may be set to go up by some known amount on a certain date. Make a note of that off to the side. It's the same with any other expense you're locked into, like maybe a merchant-account agreement for processing credit cards, or your website hosting plan, and so on.

When collecting all these details, it may be helpful to imagine that you're going to go on an adventure for a year. You need to do a brain dump of all the agreements you made in the business so your trusty deputy will be able to keep everything running properly while you're gone.

Income

In the back-pocket world we might only have thought about "what comes in." Even with the very little work we've done so far on our numbers, we're now more sophisticated. Revenue is the raw stuff that we cannot spend, because lots of expenses get taken right off the top. Revenue minus expenses equals our income.

With the details we've written down so far, you'll now start to benefit: instead of being at the squirrel/roadkill level of back-pocket accounting, you'll be able to do a bit of forecasting. Let's say it is February. With your new details about when revenue comes in and expenses go out, you can get a handle on which months have higher or lower income.

Cash Flow

There is another concept to squeeze in here, and that's cash flow. This is the true cash received after taking into account that sometimes people don't pay you on time. You might have income but you're waiting on a customer to pay; you might also have income but will put aside some of it as a reserve to pay for that big walk-in freezer you need.

What you have available after all these considerations is your spendable cash flow.

Again, I'm purposefully not getting super technical here, where other people may say "What about depreciation?" and other nuances. I'm not trying to teach proper accounting, but instead want to do one-sheet accounting—and that means avoiding tons of technical details that make business owners heave it all out the window and revert to back-pocket accounting.

100-Foot Level

Just with what we've gathered and written down here, we've made major progress. We've come up from the one-inch roadkill level to the 100-foot level. In other words, we now have a decent handle on all the money coming in, and when it arrives. We know all the money going out, and when it's due. We've taken into account any delays in receiving money and also some reserves we have set aside for big expenses coming up. I'm not talking about knowing all of this down to the penny but having a grasp of where most of the money flows.

We may be depressed at what the numbers look like, but there is still cause for a pat on the back. You're now viewing your numbers not as a hobbyist but as a businessperson. You are doing good and important work here.

Hobby Hell

I'm throwing much at you, but I'm certain that you can take it, because as a business owner, you're one of a rare and tough breed. So stick with me here.

All the stuff we've covered in this section are components of one of the two main documents in business accounting. We've been dealing with the income statement. In big-picture terms, revenue minus expenses equals income.

You can think of this as the horsepower of the business engine. If you have loads of revenue and not many expenses, then you're doing something pretty special. If you have some income, and quite a lot of expenses, then your revenue statement will sometimes show net income after expenses, or net loss after expenses.

We talked about it briefly in Chapter 2, but there is an important difference between a business and a hobby. If your business continuously runs at a loss, after a while the Internal Revenue Service will consider it to be a hobby.

You may ask: "So what?" The problem is that when the IRS considers your activity to be a hobby, you can no longer deduct business expenses from your taxes. They look at you as a dabbler in this thing that never turns a profit, so it can't benefit from taking business deductions.

This is all the more reason why you should read this book carefully and apply its recommendations. You are doing important and noble work in running a business. You deserve every tax benefit that businesses can enjoy, but you need to keep your business driving between the white lines to get them. If you veer off to the side by having no grasp of your business numbers, then you'll become roadkill in the eyes of the IRS, too.

The Balance Sheet

Okay, we've built out a serviceable income statement with all the work we've done. As a business owner, you also need a snapshot of your business's overall health and value. Accountants call this summary a balance sheet.

The balance sheet is the financial health of your business on one specific date. I can hear you thinking: *What good is that? My business runs every day and you're telling me that some document only focuses on one day?*

That's right. It's another big business concept that you should be aware of. Imagine that you drive down the main street of your town and are looking left and right at all the businesses. They have a variety of storefronts that look nice or whatever.

Now imagine that you could put on some special glasses for when you drive down the street. Those glasses apply a sort of colored overlay when you look at each business. When the business is losing money that month, the glasses show that storefront as red. When the business is running a profit that month, the glasses show green. Now that's some useful information that distinguishes those businesses.

But what about the business that just has one bad month? Maybe a business spent a bunch of money on renovations and therefore expenses were unusually high. Should that business show the same color of red that the other business does, which is constantly running a loss and is always under water?

This is where that concept of the balance sheet comes in. If your business has done well almost every month, then you'll have been able to put some money in the bank and pay off debt. In general, the business is getting stronger every month. Sure, there will be months when those magic glasses make the business look like it's in the red, but you're not worried. It's almost always in the green, so the occasional red is no big deal.

Your confidence is the balance sheet at work. You know the overall health of the business is good, so the occasional dip in performance is just that.

Here's the language of a balance sheet: you have assets, which is the stuff you own, like bank account balances, real estate, the value of machinery and equipment, and so on. Write all of these down, but don't go crazy about accounting for every last dime. Just make sure that you have the main assets written down and be sure to be realistic about the value. You may have paid $1,000 for a fancy printer or computer, but at a garage sale they are worth far less than what you paid.

Then you have liabilities, like the debt you owe to credit-card companies and to the bank for the loan, the mortgage/rent payment, or utilities bill you owe later this month. Write all of these down, just as you did for assets.

When you add up your assets on a given day and subtract the liabilities as of that day, you have the value of the business. This is the net worth of the business. Accountants call this value your "equity." That is the value you have built up in your business.

As your business grows and gets more sophisticated, accountants can help you value other intangible assets of your business, like the value of ongoing profits, the goodwill of your business, and your brand. Most small businesses don't have to contemplate any of this.

Remember that this calculation is just for one day. The reason is that accountants are very specific about what they report. We can all agree that business circumstances change constantly. I might sign a lease for extra space in one week and then get a bunch of sales in another week when we have our annual sale. At the same time, the numbers are always moving, and accounting is a profession where words like "approximately" or "more or less" are unacceptable.

Therefore, if you're trying to be accurate about what's going on in a business, you need to take a snapshot on a particular day. Everyone realizes that it's only a snapshot. When you look at a balance sheet, you'll always see a date on which that calculation was done. It's an important concept, even for one-sheet accounting.

Lengthen the Time Span

We're already way ahead of where we were, now that we have a one-sheet summary of revenues, expenses, income, and cash flow.

Before we move on to a few more key numbers, see what you can do to gather the above numbers for more than a month or two. Ideally you should have those important numbers for this month, last month, each month of this year, and each month of the past three years.

I understand if you don't have all of that information, but collect as much as you can, and enlist some help if necessary. *There is nothing more important to the growth of your business than to do this work to understand your money.* Can it be boring? Yes. Is it a pain to do, when you could be helping customers or working on some other useful task? Yes, it's a pain. But if you have not been regularly reviewing this stuff before now, then I'm sorry but you are soon to be roadkill—the only question is when it will become official. You can avoid that situation by getting this work done.

The more of a time period you can assemble these numbers for, the better you can understand what's really happening in your business. A longer period will help us to see things in the numbers, when one or two months will not provide that insight.

Let's say you have last year's monthly numbers, and it will take a little while to get the previous year's. You can start gaining insights from what you have. In other words, don't wait to collect everything and then somehow never get around to it. Work with what you have, and then work to get the rest.

A great many businesses have seasonal variations. Maybe a month in the spring and winter are traditionally the best two of the year, and another month or two can be counted upon to be the slowest.

Knowing this can help to create realistic projections, instead of inaccurately estimating that every month is like the other.

Knowing the fast and slow months also allows you to plan better to protect your business. In Episode 2 of Season 3 of SBR, identifying the slow summer months at Morrison's Irish Pub helped the owners focus on creating a plan. Morrison's created a seasonal menu that would help to attract people during those slow, warm summer months.

On the other hand, if you have months that are particularly busy, you might be able to plan further ahead to get seasonal help, or you might be able to get better discounts when you're purchasing in bulk for those months.

Ideally you should put your one-sheet document on a spreadsheet, an easy-to-use computer software. The software allows you to easily update numbers without rewriting everything. It's also a breeze to run calculations. I have two bits of good news. First, there are plenty of tutorials online on YouTube that teach you how to use the software. Second, there are many spreadsheet software choices offered by companies like Microsoft and Google. Some are available for a monthly fee, and some are available without a fee. Microsoft Excel is probably the most widely used, but Google's product Google Sheets is popular too. A simple web search will help you find spreadsheet software that fits your needs. You can also go to a service like fiverr.com and find someone to do spreadsheet modeling for you for literally $10. Just type in: "Build spreadsheet in Google Sheets" on fiverr.com and you'll see for yourself.

And if you're on your own, that's no problem. Just google "Google Sheets basics" and you'll have your pick of lots of helpful guides and videos. They'll get you up to speed in under an hour. This is time spent that will pay you back many times over.

Let's Do Some Basic Analysis

If we were sitting in the Deluxe headquarters in Minnesota, having this conversation, at this point the team would have a fundamental question for you: Are you currently paying yourself?

If you've watched even a few episodes of SBR, you know that most business owners we featured were not paying themselves a salary, or even the equivalent of minimum wage. In fact, they were doing the opposite: they had been draining their bank accounts, retirement savings, and credit cards in order to keep things afloat.

In the next chapter we talk more about the concept of paying yourself a salary. But for purposes of this chapter, what we want to do is make some calculations about that salary.

Let's say for a moment that you've either not been taking a salary or it's been far lower than it needs to be for you to consider this business-owner stuff to be a well-paid profession. What's your number? What would you like to get as a salary?

You can make two mistakes here: you can either go crazy and say, "Well, I think a million dollars is a nice, round number" (it's a great number, but we both know that it may take just a little bit of time to get there), or you could lowball yourself and say, "I'm paying myself nothing now, so even $10,000 will be a big improvement." Yes, it would, but $10,000 is not a living wage in the United States, wouldn't you agree?

If you really don't know how much to put down, then what did you earn before you started this business? You can always revisit this number, but put something down that would provide reasonably for your modest needs.

Now we're going to do our first analysis, based on the numbers you've collected so far. Of course, I don't know your business, so I cannot get specific about the product or service you sell. Therefore, I'll use a substitute, so you get the hang of it.

The case I'll use is Nyce & Clean Auto Detailing, which was *SBR* Episode 1 of Season 5. Mike Plaza is the owner, and he answered that question by smiling and saying, "I'd like to make $100,000."

So, the second question was what services Mike offered at that time. He had three services: auto detailing, window tinting, and paint correction. Now it's your turn: list your services. You should do it under the revenue section of the one-sheet, and you're going to want to know what each product or service makes.

Now if you're a store with 1,000 products, I don't mean that you should have 1,000 lines of numbers on this sheet. For now, you can roll them up. Maybe if you're a coffee shop it will be beverages, baked items, sandwiches, and something else. If you are an attorney, it might be that you have some package deals like doing the website legal work for $1,000 per site. Perhaps you have a different offering where you

Mike wants revenue to be this per year: $100,000

	Price to Customer	Volume per Month	Revenue per Month	Revenue per Year
Auto detailing	$100	16	$1,600	$19,200
Window tinting	$220	20	$4,400	$52,800
Paint buffing	$150	10	$1,500	$18,000

Total Mike expects to see: $90,000

Figure 3.1   How much Mike can expect to bring in per year

charge $200 per hour. If it's a service you do somewhat regularly, then put that down as a line item.

In Mike's case at Nyce & Clean, the third question was what he charged for each service. The fourth question was how long each service took Mike to do, broken out by each service. Next, Mike estimated how many of each service he thought he'd see in a 30-day period.

Now it's a matter of simple multiplication. This is where the spreadsheet makes things far easier than manual calculations, because spreadsheets shine at "what-if" scenarios. You can load in your price per service, number of sales of each service per month, and then project that for the whole year. Figure 3.1 shows what that looks like for the entire year for Mike.

Now we're getting into some good thinking about Mike's business. First, Mike wants to make $100,000 per year, but when he estimates how many of each service he'll do in a year, it totals $90,000.

If Mike's estimates are good, then he'll fall short of his goal by $10,000. But having a spreadsheet like this enables Mike to think hard about his volume and pricing. What if Mike can do 22 window tintings per month instead of 20? Once the spreadsheet is built, he can literally change the 20 to a 22 in one second and see the result, shown in Figure 3.2.

Mike wants revenue to be this per year: $100,000

	Price to Customer	Volume per Month	Revenue per Month	Revenue per Year
Auto detailing	$100	16	$1,600	$19,200
Window tinting	$220		$4,840	$58,080
		22		
Paint buffing	$150	10	$1,500	$18,000

Total Mike expects to see: ↖
$95,280

Figure 3.2   What happens if Mike does two more tintings per month

Now maybe you can do complicated spreadsheets in your sleep. That's great, but I don't want to assume something like that. I can tell you that if Mike is new to spreadsheets, if he gets to this stage of building his first business model, he's going to be one excited dude.

Why? Because he's stepping back from working *in* the business and finally is able to work *on* the business and do some good thinking around pricing and goals. He can do a ton of what-if analyses in a short period:

That boost to 22 tints per month now has me at $95,000 per year. What if I can do a couple more paint buffings per month? But window tinting is a lot more profitable than detailing so maybe I can cut back on the time-consuming detailing and get more tint jobs in. What would that look like?. . .

Mike can easily get as complex as he'd like. For example, he might remember that he's had a fourth service in the past, and he could add that to the spreadsheet. Or he may decide to bust out the volume number into 12 columns so he can really project his high-volume months and slow months with more accuracy.

Note how this spreadsheet is only looking at revenue and not income after expenses. That's another enhancement Mike can make to the model: add columns for what each service costs him in materials and labor. He might conclude that he could hire someone to do some of these services, which would free him up to do the most profitable ones himself.

This is where Mike's brain catches on fire in other ways, too: he remembers that some people have asked him for types of super detailing that he can do and could charge an even higher price. Now he can model these additional services by adding a row and playing around with the price and volume numbers.

On the other hand, he may realize that a service is taking way too much of his time for the money he makes, and he'd want to model what happens if he dropped that service to zero volume six months from now and boosted the volume of a different service. Even if Mike is new to spreadsheets, that sort of adjustment will take only about five minutes.

The additional beauty of Google Sheets is that it automatically saves your work, and if you mess up some numbers, it allows you to undo any changes, as far back as you like.

Now that you've spent some time on the most important question of what your business needs to do in order for you to get paid properly, let's look at other key numbers.

Cost of Goods Sold

The term "cost of goods sold" (COGS) may sound like some obscure accounting concept, but it's really important for many small businesses: it's the direct cost of supplies and labor you need to produce what you sell. It does not include indirect labor like management, nor does it include things like rent.

In Season 4, Episode 7, we saw that the owners of Savor + Sip Coffeehouse were paying retail for food to use in the store. That was a huge realization, because stores that sell food are already operating on tight profit margins. In order to make ends meet, they needed to buy their ingredients at much lower costs. Fortunately, if you google the term "Wholesale food suppliers," you should find a number of companies that want your business.

Another issue relating to COGS came up in Season 2, Episode 2 where an entirely different type of business had an issue. In this case it was the auto-repair shop, Hems. When the owners came to Minnesota to talk with the Deluxe team, it became apparent that they were getting auto parts from only one supplier. Robert Herjavec lit up at that news.

Even though it might seem logical to concentrate your purchasing through one supplier in the hope that you get a good deal, it often does not work out that way. In your personal life, you understand this. When you shop at the grocery store, you know the sale items are usually at a very low price. But you pick up items not on sale on the same shopping trip just because it's easy. You know you could probably get a lower price on some of those nonsale items if you shopped around.

It's the same in business. If a supplier thinks you're not shopping around for the best price, you might get a few good prices, but you'll likely also get some pretty bad prices too. If suppliers know they must compete for your business, that's a different matter. Robert added: "Every dollar you save off the cost of goods goes right into your pocket."

You may be thinking: *I wish I had Amanda and Robert in my corner, but I don't.* That's true, but never fear—the solution is just a Google search away. If you are a restaurant, you can google the phrase "cost of goods for restaurant" and you'll see some great results that break down the numbers you should be shooting for.[3] But let's say you're in a completely different industry, like being a florist. Even so, you can quickly find good information on what your costs should be.[4]

Let's say that you have a highly technical question about your particular industry and have not been able to find an answer. You should check out an interesting site that allows people to ask any question under the sun and get answers. There are many sites that can help, but a popular one is quora.com. Although it's true that sometimes the answers will not be from experts, often they will be from people who really do know what they're talking about in your industry or community. As with anything on the web, you have to separate the good stuff from everything else.

After you've done some analysis on your COGS, you should consider adding that information to your spreadsheet. In the case of Mike, the owner of auto detailer Nyce & Clean, he started out with virtually no cost of goods sold: he cleaned cars with a brush, rag, spray bottle, and bucket. But when Mike decided to get into the window-tinting business, now he had to buy the window film, among other expenses.

If Mike modifies his spreadsheet, he can do some interesting analyses. For example, what if he could buy decent window film at a lower cost? What would his income after expenses be if he can lower the COGS on the tinting? On the other hand, Mike may know his competition and he may decide that most of them are using low-cost inferior window films, and he can talk up the premium stuff he uses. Maybe his supplier has testimonials from a couple of National Football League players who say they only use that film on their cars. Mike can decide to spend the extra money for the premium film, but he may also decide to two-tier pricing: regular film and super-premium. Let the customers decide which one they want. Over time, Mike may load in the actual sales to his model and decide that he'll kill off the regular film and only stock the premium product because 90 percent of his customers want it and are willing to pay the premium price. Or he may find that the reverse is true.

We have just seen how you can literally take a free tool like Google Sheets and develop the beginnings of a business model. The more details you load in about your costs and sales, the more questions you can ask and answers you can get. For example: Where do I make most of my money? What might I expect to see if I offer this other product? How many units do I need to sell in order to have enough revenue to hire a part-time person?

Early in this chapter I suggested that you load in as much data about previous months as you can get your hands on. I hope you can see how that *past* data can be useful in predicting *future* events. If you know that in the past three years you've never done less than $X in sales of something, that may give you some confidence about what your minimum results will be. And once you see the value of this modeling effort, you'll be adding more and more data into the spreadsheet. That will in turn give you an ever-stronger foundation for further planning.

What's Your Capacity and True Market Demand?

Some small businesses have very elastic capacity, meaning they have the ability to do much more business easily. Others don't. In other words, for some businesses, like online coaching or online yoga, there's no upper limit to the number of students that can attend a class. However, many businesses do have clear limits, before they need to get more space, more employees, or both.

In Season 2, Episode 7, we heard about the daycare center "Discover Learn & Grow—Early Learning Center." Ramona Jones and her son, Marcelous Jones, own a great example of a business with a clear maximum capacity. They want to provide really quality care for children, and they know how many kids can be cared for by how many staff members.

In situations like theirs, a spreadsheet can be helpful for planning. They could create another small spreadsheet that contains the number of children and different fees that families pay. For example, some families may pay the full amount, but others have a different arrangement. The spreadsheet should show all the different arrangements, and how many children are in each type. That almost takes care of the revenue side of the spreadsheet.

I said "almost" because here's an important concept. *Your spreadsheet must reflect reality, not wishful thinking, both on the capacity of your business and the demand for your services.*

It is incredibly important to be realistic about how much opportunity there is in your community for your service. Many owners significantly overestimate the potential market size, projecting what they think the market should demand, rather than what it really does demand. This is a natural mistake, as every business owner naturally loves their business and thinks everyone else should too.

In order to determine the market size for a child care center, for example, you would need to know how many children are in the area. How many have working parents and will need regular or part-time care? Is your facility in a convenient location and easy for parents to drop off/pick up before and after work? How does your location and facility compare to the competition's? Honestly, would you select your offering over your competitors' and why? Adding up your answers to all of these questions can help you roughly determine the market opportunity.

Now let's talk about managing capacity. For example, let's say an exercise studio sold 100 memberships but only 71 are at full fee; 20 are at half the fee, and the other 9 have promised to pay but you're chasing them. The spreadsheet should reflect actual dollars collected. A promise to pay or interest in joining are not the same as cash in your hand. Your spreadsheet needs to reflect actual received (or could realistically be received) revenue so you can project accurately.

Next let's take a theoretical daycare center where you have determined there are 120 children with families that could be interested in your service. The three full-time people and one half-time person collectively are able to care for a maximum of 65 children, and they have 58 enrolled at various fee levels. This means they have room to add 7 more children with their current resources. With a total universe of 120 available children, adding those additional children to their facility seems achievable on the surface. Obviously, if there are other comparable centers that collectively (including yours) have capacity for 200 children, but there are only 120 available children/families, adding 7 more might be considerably more difficult.

It's now easy to do some math and run two scenarios.

Scenario 1: We know on average that the fees we collect are $150 per month, and we have seven vacancies. We're currently bringing in 65 kids at an average of $150 per month, or $9,750. If we fill those vacant slots at our average fee, that's an additional 7 times $150, or $1,050. At our average fee, the facility will bring in $9,750 + 1,050 or $10,800.

Scenario 2: We want to know the maximum that this facility can earn us. Therefore we'll take the full 65 slots times the full fee of $200, or $13,000.

To summarize, if all seats are filled, the likely revenue of that facility is $10,800 and the maximum is $13,000. Now the owners are in a better position to determine whether the business is likely to meet their goals they may have set for paying themselves.

Building a spreadsheet like this is so powerful because it starts to show you what options you have in your business in your market. Do you have unused space? In that case, how many more memberships or products can you sell? Is there enough demand for your product or service that you can actually sell more? If so, maybe there is space next door: if you know the cost of that space, then you can work out how many additional products or services you'll need to sell in order to cover the additional lease payment.

You can do the opposite with spreadsheets as well. In Season 3, Episode 3, we met Benjamin Golley, who owned Today's Beauty Supply. Benjamin knew his inventory well and concluded that about 20 percent of the items on his shelves did not sell. This would be another time to fire up the spreadsheet and do some modeling. What if Benjamin replaced that static inventory and gave more space to his best-selling lines? What might that do to his revenues without raising prices or increasing his expenses? He'd be doing what the most sophisticated retailers on the planet do—he'd be optimizing his shelf space.

Golden Ratios

The initial nuisance of gathering all those historical numbers—and it is a nuisance—will now pay off in other ways. When you have these basic numbers about where you bring in money and where you spend it, now you can run some calculations.

SBR highlighted Tracy and Aaron Griffith in their store Thriftalicious in Season 1, Episode 6. One of the first things that struck Robert was the huge space they were paying for. Robert said that in his experience, the number-one metric for knowing how your business is doing when you have a retail physical store is sales per square foot.

Sometimes businesses are bursting out of a tiny store and need to get more space in order to be profitable. Sometimes the opposite is true: you need to try to shed space—and rent—because you have more space than you need in order to showcase your products profitably. It's like running your business with a heavy backpack on. At Deluxe we reduced our real estate locations by 60 percent for this very reason.

A spreadsheet allows you to model different scenarios of smaller space, lower rent, any penalties for getting out of a lease early, revenue from subleasing space, and how many of these various factors might end up on the bottom line.

SCORE Mentoring Program

You need to know about another resource: it's at score.org. It's tempting—and sometimes justified—to dump on the government as a waste of taxpayer money. However, in the case of the Small Business Administration, they do a pretty good job. One of the initiatives they support is the SCORE Mentoring Program.

This is a service that has helped more than 11 million businesses over the decades. They have a lot of online resources, but they also can hook you up with personal mentors. These people are often very experienced owners of businesses, who for whatever reason want to give back to other business owners.

This service is free, and you should visit and bookmark them as a solid, helpful resource.

~~~

Now that we've done some heavy lifting on the numbers side, let's look at some of the many other factors at work in your business, with an eye to improving those too.

4

Concentric Circles

In The Previous chapters, we have been able to do a substantial amount of deep thinking about your business. We covered a basic set of key numbers to get us off the roadkill level and up to that 100-foot level of perspective. Then we looked at some of the realities and decisions that face business owners, and how to navigate them.

Now we're going to continue the important discussion of your business, and we'll do that by figuratively drawing concentric circles starting with you, the driver of your business enterprise, and going out to everyone else who's involved in it.

We will look at many aspects of your business in order to see what works, what does not work, and even what does not exist.

It's important to go into this with the right frame of mind. The wrong one would be: *Wow, that was depressing! Here I wanted to get some cheerleading and to feel better about my business, and what I've come away with is this long list of things to focus on. Ugh.*

I want to introduce you to a concept that I'll occasionally use in this book; it's called the "grown-up moment." You really do have to have the tough skin of a grown-up to be a business owner. Some business owners feel a little bit lonely at times, flying solo in this whole matter of running and growing a business. Maybe you also feel that way. If only you had a coach who's been where you are now and who could give you advice that you could trust.

No book can quite match having a live, experienced business coach who will take the time to walk you through the key decisions you need to make as a business owner. If you have such a person, then congrats. But if you do not, then this book is the next best thing.

Therefore, in the spirit of a grown-up moment, I want to say that if you want an unconditional cheerleader to make you feel better, get a dog. My goal is not to make you feel better about what your business is currently doing, but instead to help your business do better, by giving you guidance about how to navigate those seismic events that we talked about earlier.

As you are already painfully aware, building a small business is not for the faint of heart. It's a daily challenge where the buck stops with you. Therefore, you don't need some fortune cookie at this stage that will tell you it will all turn out okay. Instead, you need a guide that will highlight what you need to do—and stop doing—in order for it to turn out fine.

The right frame of mind therefore is to go through the remaining chapters of this book and think: *Wow, that was eye-opening! Here I thought all I wanted was some cheerleading, but that's not what I got. I can't deposit "high-fives" at the bank. What I need are "top fives" in the sense of a handful of key areas I need to focus on and change in order to grow my business.*

Helping you focus on what's needed to succeed—that's my goal in these chapters.

About You

What keeps you up at night? I don't mean the barking dog next door, though you might want to get that soundproofing. Instead, we want to identify on paper the underlying, fundamental root cause of what keeps you up at night about your business.

By the way, I strongly suggest that you get out some paper for what we're going to do here. I'm sure you have a fine memory, and you may like to think by discussing things and not writing them down. What I've found is that the act of writing has a way of forcing your brain to choose more precise words, and to be clear and honest. It makes it harder to hide from a truth you may not want to accept. You write a thought, then decide that it's not quite right and scratch it out and restate it. That's an important process that's not effectively done without looking at the words.

Back to that root cause: what we want to identify here are not outcomes but causes, as specifically as we can. For example, an outcome would be to say "My business sucks" or "I'm not making enough money." Try to list as many situations as you can that are tough decisions, or unresolved pressures. They might even be comments others have made about your business.

- One business owner will say it's because they're getting killed by the big-box store that set up shop on the outskirts of town.
- Another owner will say that it's because things are always feast or famine: in the winter months their tavern is full and they turn away people, and in the summer months they can't get enough people.
- An owner could know that he needs to specialize but can't bring himself to do it. He gets some business from parents who bring their kids to get great training. But the facility also attracts very serious people who could become world-class, if the owner takes the time to coach them. The business already operates at break-even, so the owner is highly resistant to any specialization. After all, that will mean moving away from some current revenue, even if it potentially means becoming more focused and more attractive to one segment.
- In a similar way, an owner may have a business name that's very meaningful to him. The problem is that no one else loves the name, and in fact it is confusing to customers, who spell things one way while the owner insists on spelling things another way.
- An owner may admit that her business is in a much bigger space than is necessary for now and for the foreseeable future. But she insists that "someday" we'll be glad we have all that space, when the business is booming.
- An owner is adamant about not trying something that could bring in revenue. He *will never* offer a free sample of something because he believes it is insulting to give away something of value.

- An owner cares extremely passionately about her friends, who were there at the beginning. In fact, they drew the original logo for the business. People have delicately hinted at how the logo may no longer be the best for the business, but the owner feels like it would disrespect the friends to *ever* change the logo.

These are all situations that owners have faced in SBR episodes. I suggest that you keep a running list of the items you identify in your business, and also ask others for their opinion. Sometimes it takes time for your subconscious mind to bubble up all the issues you've thought of before.

We will get into much greater detail about all of this, but I want to start with those lead weights you are carrying around in that invisible backpack of yours—you know, the one that's embroidered with "For Business Owners Only."

About Your Co-Workers

I chose the term "co-workers" carefully because of the realities of small businesses. You may be the owner, but I bet you've been "chief cook and bottle washer," as they say, at times. There may be other owners, and maybe a big dose of family members and helpers in the mix as well. It could even be that kids younger than employment age are helping out with tasks informally.

If you take all of that into account, it's important to think about what's working, what's kind of not working, and what is definitely not working.

If I look back over the dozens of episodes of SBR, here are some of the issues that relate to co-workers:

- There is more than one owner, but they each bring different things to the table. One person has the specialized knowledge that the business needs and is the creative one. The other person has almost exclusively funded the business. So, is one owner more crucial or senior to the other? How do disputes get resolved?
- A business experiences some strain because one of the key family members has to commute a long way to work elsewhere in order to make ends meet. The goal is to have her work in the business.

- Another business experiences pretty much the opposite: all family members work or hang out at the business, and this is not by choice. It's because the owners can't afford to have their kids at an early learning center.
- Someone in the family has bankrolled the business and in a sense is holding the business hostage. He's controlling the books until the real owners are "ready"—whatever that means—to take on all the financial responsibilities. This means that the people running daily operations are running it blindly.
- There are two owners of the business, but no documents that lay out who owns what. Things are usually worked out after discussions or heated arguments, but no one emerges unscathed. What if things go downhill from here?
- The owner thinks he can run the business but everyone around him realizes that he has no management skills. They've tried to hint at how he should bring in someone, but the response is always "That's not necessary. I'm good."
- The owner is in fact great at conducting classes, so he spends a lot of time doing just that. The problem is that other parts of the business are suffering, because they're technically being run by the owner, who's ignoring them and is off teaching more classes.
- The most common situation of all: the owners are working themselves to the bone, doing everything. They may have no one to do their job, so that means no weekends or vacations to rest. Ever. If it were for a few months, then no big deal. But this situation sometimes goes on *for years*.

Do you see your situation in any of these? Even if you don't, maybe you have some other dynamics at work. Again, I suggest that you write them down. Depending on the degree of openness at your business, maybe it would be helpful to talk about this with others—or maybe not. Even if it's just a matter of your own private thoughts, that's fine for now.

One point that may be helpful: the choice of words matters when you're thinking about any issues that are less than great. Labels are not as helpful as desired states. This is especially true if you're going to try to sit down with someone and resolve an issue. But it's also true even if you're just thinking on paper.

For example, you may have had a long history with someone and the way you'd honestly describe the situation is: "I wish Bill wasn't such a total jerk"—except your true feelings might be represented by words stronger than "jerk."

What I suggest you instead do is think about the specific actions that justify labeling Bill as a jerk. Maybe it is: "I cannot think of a single time in the past year when Bill took anyone else's advice. He insists that his opinions are the only correct ones, and that's even after some really bad outcomes when he didn't take other people's recommendations. And they were right while Bill was wrong."

That's so much more useful. It also focuses on Bill's actions and not on him as a human being. Now I get that maybe he doesn't deserve to have his feelings considered, if he never cares about others. Even so, if you state the action ("not taking anyone else's advice") and quantify the action ("not once in the past year"), now you may have the basis for a discussion.

Maybe you're wrong about Bill, and he would say: "Hey, wait a minute; I took Sergei's advice about our May event, and I took Chantal's advice about our front window display." If you're focused on specifics, then it's easier for people to have to agree, or else come up with specifics of their own.

Have a Sandwich

You may or may not know this time-tested technique, and I will mention that there isn't universal agreement about its effectiveness, but I find it is easy to use and especially helpful when you're trying to deliver a sensitive or difficult message to someone who may not be receptive. The idea is simple: where possible, put a negative trait or aspect in the center, surrounded by two positive ones, sandwich style.

Here's what that looks like:

You know, Andy, there is no one better than you at troubleshooting problems when customers come in with their cameras. What I've seen at least a couple of people complain about in our Google reviews—and I've also seen it happen myself—is you'll talk down to them sometimes. You'll say stuff like: "Let me educate you on the difference between Nikon and Canon lenses" or "That's a real beginner mistake you made to not set the ISO on the camera to Auto." If you can just give them the advice without using any talking-down terms, then we'll get fewer negative reviews. And we both know that you'll still be the most knowledgeable camera tech in all of Philly.

The reason this model works is that the opening positive point is making it clear you value the other person and are providing a genuine and sincere compliment. In this way, you are clearly not complaining, you are genuinely offering a suggestion for improvement. Then closing with a compliment affirms your respect for and confidence in them.

You should know that some people don't like the sandwich—they would just prefer to be hit on the head with the message. Your job will be to determine how best to deliver the message so it is heard and accepted.

Testing, Testing

Another frequently effective way to change things is to position them as a test. This is especially helpful when you suggest something, and you get the good old "it'll never work" response, or the "I tried that in the 1990s and it didn't work then, and it won't work now."

You could say: "You may be absolutely right; but sometimes circumstances change. If we run a test either for a short time, or on just a portion of our customers, we'll soon see what happens."

You really should consider this concept even when the one making the objection is you. If you're reluctant to do something, for whatever reason, think about how you could test it, to find out for sure.

Your Brand

The word "brand" often sends the wrong message when working with small businesses. It's easy for a business owner to think: *Coca-Cola . . . now that's a brand. Known the world over. I'm just Frank's Pizza Palace. That's not really a "brand" but just a business. I don't even spend any money on my "brand."*

You Have One, Whether You Know It or Not

Every business indeed has a brand, though. Let's take the used-car lot on the edge of town. It always has a couple of junkers on a tow truck, parked nearby. All cars on the lot have prices scrawled in fat, white paint on each window. And when you walk by the open garage, it looks dark, disorganized, and dirty. Without spending a dime, the owner of this business has a well-known brand throughout town.

If you ask J.C., the used-car lot owner, about his brand he'll probably say either "I don't waste time on that stuff" or "It's quality used cars." The strange thing is that J.C. might indeed pride himself on great used cars, but the cosmetic part of his brand is at odds with the automotive part.

What Your Brand Is Not

Let's clarify something right up front, because lots of people make a mistake here: your logo is not your brand.

Think of your logo as your foot in the door to people's awareness. It could be when someone's walking down the street with your retail packaging and your logo is on it. The logo of course can be in many other places like postcards, pens, and so on. We'll talk more about promotional products later. Your logo is an important identifier of the larger statement, which is the brand you have or create.

When branding is done right, it encompasses how the surroundings make your customers feel when they walk into your retail shop or online store. Do they get a modern, trendy feel? Or when they walk in, do they get a rustic farmhouse feel, or a homey one where they feel like they're wrapped in a hug? Your brand strategy needs to be this sort of broader conversation, and ideally you have it before you design a logo.

We met Whilma Frogoso in Season 4, Episode 2. She brought her father's Filipino recipes from the Philippines to Searcy, Arkansas, and the food in her restaurant was super-authentic. She needed a brand to be just as authentic. The Deluxe team worked on the logo, but also focused on colors that would be true to Filipino traditions. Part of the brand included pictures on the wall of Whilma's parents—an inspiration to her and a message about how this relatively new restaurant is carrying on an old tradition.

What Is Your Brand, Then?

Let's start with your opinion: What do you want to be known for? What feelings do you want to generate in the minds of customers? They can run the gamut from the warm hug in a clothing store to goth, heavy-metal, end-of-the-world stuff in a music store, or perhaps high-tech and Spartan in a dermatology clinic. Write down your initial thoughts, whatever they are. Go ahead; I'll wait.

Let's take a look at what you wrote. I hope you didn't dust off your mission statement here. Those documents have their place, but when done incorrectly, they also can become meaningless pretty quickly.

For example, if you get enough suits around a table, you're liable to get group agreement on something that uses terms like "synergy," "acknowledged global leader," and "value maximization."

I'm sorry, but when your significant other turns to you and says "Where should we go to eat tonight?" you are highly unlikely to say "Well, honey, I think we should go to that place on the corner that strives to create a synergistic, win/win environment for all of its stakeholders through world-class leadership delivering value maximization." Unless you want to eat alone.

The next thing to do is ask other people in your business to write down what they think you want to be known for. I suggest you ask them to do this individually and not as a group. Invariably there will be some alpha person who's the loudest with his opinions and others who are willing to go along to get along. What you should look for are individual opinions. Tell them that you're not looking for polished prose, but just ideas. They may not even be whole sentences, but just phrases or individual words.

Next, ask your customers, because their opinions count the most on this topic—*even more than your own*. It may be your business, but it's their wallets and they determine whether they open them for you or go to a competitor.

It could be that this exercise will clarify what you want your brand to engender in your customers' minds. It could also be that all this information serves to make you more confused than ever. In that case, you might consider getting outside help.

First, you can google "brand strategy" and find useful questions and checklists. If you want to talk with a specialist, you may wonder: *How can I find someone who doesn't cost a fortune, and will help me to work through all of this?*

A good place to start is with your town's business association or the Chamber of Commerce. If you ask around, you may find a business owner who's quite happy with the branding work someone did. Also, you'll be able to see the brand of that business for yourself and determine if it's in the quality and cost ballpark you had in mind.

What It's Like to Work with a Good Brand Specialist

Here's a tip that can save you a lot of grief. It can be useful to have an expert help you through this business-building activity, but you need to be clear about what you're looking for. Sometimes people say they want a branding specialist when all they're really after is a logo. Other times, people think that a new logo is all they need to improve the positioning of their business, when in fact they need the full brand review. From reading this chapter, you already know enough to not confuse the two.

If you do decide to look for someone to help you with the larger brand discussion, you don't want a rubber-stamp type who will think all your ideas are fabulous. What you need is someone whom you'll respect for his or her expertise, but also someone who gets you.

For example, you might have a great emotional attachment to the color pink. People may tell you that your personality is hot pink, and you're loud and out-there about it. A good brand specialist is going to do research about your products, existing customers, and the target market of potential customers. The specialist should explain how the best brands do two things: they reflect the personality of the business and its owner on the one hand and, more importantly, appeal to the personality of the target market on the other.

It could be that hot pink works great for you, the owner, but may be driving away customers. One thing that you didn't see in the *SBR* series is that the customer-experience team at Deluxe would spend a lot of time identifying and interviewing the top customers of businesses. We'd show them different designs to see which ones resonated the most. If they discovered, for instance, that hot pink was not what those customers cared for, a good brand expert could usually find a middle ground appealing to all.

Logos

Maybe you will have this person help you with a new logo. How do you even know when to get a new logo? One good time is when your business has grown or changed substantially.

For example, maybe you started an Etsy store and quickly built it up to 200 different items for sale. Over time, you discovered that only about 30 of those products made you any real money. The others were tying up your cash in inventory. If you look at the 30 winning products, perhaps you would see that there's a theme in common, and a new logo could reinforce the theme.

Good designers will first do the legwork I just described. Then they'll create different versions of the logo: one might very closely reflect what customers liked the most; another one is what the designer thinks is closest to what the owner will love; and one version would be in between the two.

It's a good move for the designer first to present the logos in black and white. That way you can determine what you like strictly about the design, not influenced by colors. Then once you settle on the black-and-white design, there can be another round of options for colors using that design.

If you can't yet afford a branding consultant to help you with your logo, there are many low-cost web-based services that can help you develop a quality logo design quickly. Some include Wordpress.com, Squarespace, Web.com, and of course our own website by design at Deluxe.com.

Mood Boards

In many *SBR* episodes, you saw that our designers created a mood board with the help of the owner. It's a place where photographs, fabrics, and maybe other materials come together to give you an impression of what the owner is trying to achieve with a brand. These can be useful, because they can be shown to all the parties I've mentioned: "Does this set of items and images convey what we're trying to do here?" If not, it can be adjusted. If it does accurately convey the feeling, then the board will be a good reference for the work that follows. When elements of the brand get created like the logo and promotional items, they can be compared to the mood board to see if they appear to clash or fit in.

There's nothing stopping you from creating a mood board right away. In fact, a good, free approach is to create a Pinterest board. As you may know, Pinterest is organized as a series of cards with images and text. You can mix and match them and keep the board as private or public as you wish. Start collecting examples of how you would like your business to be perceived. It will help you, whether you hire a specialist or not.

Your Brand as a Choice

Let's say you think you're known for the best plumbing parts selection in the state, but most people will say that they go to you for the best advice from service people. In that case, you can avoid sinking even more money into plumbing parts inventory when you should be hiring more great service techs.

Part of the brand objective is to own a phrase in the heads of your target market, and to be accurate about what that phrase is. In Season 3, Episode 2, Morrison's Irish Pub had several contenders for what it could be known for. The owners, Lisa Morrison, Mary Morrison, and Katey Vankirk, prided themselves on tasting and curating more than 60 Irish whiskeys.

Then again, they baked everything from scratch. Plus, it was clear from the episode that an important draw was live Irish music, with customers really enjoying the act of singing along, judging by the looks on people's faces. Oh, and their prices for whiskeys and beers were surprisingly low.

It's certainly possible that if you said: "Where should we go to eat tonight?," your buddy would say: "Let's go to Morrison's—they always pick up my mood at the end of the week with their singalongs." In a sense, that's perfect, because it is an image in the mind of this customer and it's easily and effectively conveyed in a few words.

Then again, someone else may say: "They bake a brown soda bread that is even better than what I used to get in County Cork, Ireland." Another person will rave about the whiskey selection. Someone else will say that Morrison's has the lowest-cost brews around, and other people will find something else that they love.

The thing is, you cannot be all things to all people. No brand can be that. McDonald's is known for tasty beef burgers, consistent quality, all fairly priced with quick service. It's not trying to compete with the fancy Japanese restaurant down the street selling ultra-premium Kobe beef with leisurely paced service and extremely high prices. Every business has to make their choices and become known for them.

Fortunately, you can rely on an old Italian guy to help you grow your business. His name is Vilfredo Pareto. Now Vilfredo may have died back in 1923, but a principle he created is still relevant nearly 100 years later.[1] His "Pareto principle" is also known as the "80/20 Rule." In other words, 80 percent of something is usually due to 20 percent of something else. In practice, this may mean that 20 percent of our menu items represent 80 percent of our revenues.

Almost everyone misunderstands this principle and thinks that the numbers have to add up to 100. In practice, the Pareto principle could mean that 78 percent of sales at Morrison's Irish Pub are from only 10 percent of the menu items. Or it could be that 90 percent of sales are from 23 percent of items.

The big takeaway from this principle is the concept of the "vital few." Morrison's is known for a number of great things, but the Pareto principle predicts that it's not due to everything they're known for equally.

Therefore, if the owners ask enough people, they'll start to get a sense that the low cost of beers is not nearly as important as the live music. Or it might be that the music is fine, but the real draw is that people come from 50 miles away to sample the broad selection of Irish whiskeys.

This is your assignment, and it can be hard work. For your business, you need to find out the vital few things you are doing that represent the main reasons why they like to pay you money. It *will not* be the case that all of your products and services are equally valued. Importantly, what you want those factors to be is entirely irrelevant. The only thing that matters is what is important to your customer. That's all that matters.

You may push back and say: "Why do we have to limit what we do? Why can't Morrison's be all those different things to all those different groups of people?" That's a good question!

Fortunately, I have a good answer. Unless you're Steve Jobs and you are unveiling the world's first smartphone, you likely operate on thin margins. Your competitors have a lot of what you have, though maybe not everything. Therefore, you need to specialize and be good at something very specific to be successful and gain market share. If you're well known for just a few things, then you will stand apart from the people who kind of, sort of do a lot of things. They have a few whiskeys, and their prices are okay. They have live music once a month and their muffins are homemade but everything else is not made from scratch. Or, their food and beer are cheap; I would never bring a date there.

Reduce Risk by Testing

Earlier we talked about how powerful it can be to position changes as merely a test to see if something works. The same is true here. We could write up a super-simple survey in which we ask a bunch of customers about what they care about the most: low beer prices, live music, everything baked from scratch, the widest selection of Irish whiskeys, and maybe a few other items we come up with.

If we survey a couple dozen customers, we will not get back responses that equally rank those factors, so we can focus on the top three or so features. Let's try emphasizing our live music, fresh-baked items, and whiskey selection. And because we think they're less important, let's increase prices on beer and whiskey by a dollar or so. We can't run a test over one week, because that's too short a period. We might have had a big snowstorm that week, so not many customers showed up to begin with. But if we look at results over several weeks, we should be able to draw some conclusions.

Remember that the whole idea of helping Morrison's Irish Pub is to find some way to keep customers happy, while enabling the super-hard-working owners and staff to stay in business and earn a living wage, or even a little more. That means making some choices that will bring in more money with the same work, or more money with less work. The test will tell us.

Maybe we start by raising prices on beer and whiskey and see how that affects the number of customers and our profitability. Let's say we see a steep drop-off, and people are complaining about the price increases. In that case, we can make a big deal of bringing prices back down to our level of 10 years ago, and we can try something else.

Maybe our surveys of people found that few mentioned the live music, or it was outranked by other things. If so, we could gingerly back off of the number of live-music days, save that expense, and try turning Tuesday nights into recorded music of customer-requested Irish oldies. Morrison's could curate the largest number of recorded Irish tunes anywhere.

What does that do to our revenues? We can always reinstate the live music if we see a clear drop-off. That won't affect the loyal customer base any more than if we had to close briefly because the Alton, Illinois downtown area got flooded—which has happened. We might even find that people sing along as much or even more when there's a wide selection of recorded music. If not, customers will be glad that they return to the old arrangement. They'll not be insulted that Morrison's tried something else, any more than they'd be angry if there is a test entree on the menu that may or may not become a fan favorite over time.

Experimentation is incredibly important. We can sit around and insist that of course customers will prefer live music. Or we can find out for sure. The same is true with every other business. Let me restate this: I'm here to tell you in one respect, every business is the same. Whether you're Apple or you sell apples on a pushcart somewhere, you will benefit by testing. Relying exclusively on your own thoughts will not lead you to success—you must talk to your customers regularly and test different things to increase your odds of success.

In Season 3, Episode 4, we met Alicia Jeffreys at her Shampooches dog-grooming business. She knew about pet-taxi services, doggie daycare, and boarding, but hadn't been offering them. Alicia was hesitant about some of them, thinking that the dogs may not enjoy the experience.

But the great thing about Alicia was that she was upfront and there to listen to the expert Deluxe brought in, Jennifer Bishop-Jenkins. Alicia could have insisted that she knew her dog customers better than anyone, and that those services were not right for her specific business. Instead, she tested them and the services made a big difference to her bottom line.

I'll give you three other things to keep in mind with testing.

First, circumstances change. Even if you tried something years ago, it may be worth trying again. We need look no further than the COVID hell that we've been through to know that things can profoundly change in a hurry. Our world turned inside out and some things will not be returning to the way they were. Don't let yourself get stuck in the mindset that because you tried something once, it's now off-limits for eternity.

Second, do not call winners and losers too early. This is a major mistake that businesses make. For example, let's say you wanted to run a test and you sent 50 customers one type of promotion for Mother's Day. At the same time, you sent a different promotion with different pictures and maybe a larger discount to 50 other customers. You made five sales from one group and seven sales from the other. Did one promotion win? No, it did not. A flip of a coin could account for that amount of difference.

I won't get into detail here, but lots of businesses mistake randomness for insights. If I toss a coin 10 times and get seven heads, I should not conclude that the coin is rigged, or that I'm especially gifted or lucky. Now if I tossed a coin 1,000 times and got 700 heads, that would be remarkable, because things like 7 in 10 tend to even out when you do something 1,000 times.

This is all to say that when you test a new approach, you should feel confident of the results only if there's a huge difference between the two variations, or if you've tested it over a large number of people or over a long period of time.

The third point is that you should always be testing something. This is a huge secret to getting better—and more profitable—over time. There is no end to the sorts of things you can test: prices, discounts, bundled products, different ads (in Google, Facebook, or in your local newspaper), new services, new flavors, different operating hours, takeout options, and so on. I don't know your particular business, but I can say with a high degree of confidence that your competition is not testing. If you test regularly and properly, you will eat their lunch.

~~~

We have done some hard thinking about the people in our business, and also what we want to be known for. Now it's time to take those insights and make sure that the world knows about them.

5

Getting Visible

I Suspect You'd agree that there is no shortage of information online about how to get online. This chapter won't cover those basics that everyone seems to get. What I do want to go over are 16 common mistakes that business owners make with their online presence. They are not putting their best foot forward for their business, and in some cases don't have any foot out there at all. Other mistakes relate to taking online risks that could sink their business.

The second part of this chapter is about two big visibility boosters you can employ to build your business or get through slow times.

16 Common Mistakes Business Owners Make with Their Online Presence

Mistake #1: Not Having a Website to Begin With

I understand how this can happen. You've convinced yourself that your existing customers don't care about the web and so why bother with a website. The problem: today, most new customers find a business through web search.

Maybe you participate in social-media sites without having your own proprietary site. Many social-media sites encourage businesses to set up shop with them for free. They also make it quite easy to have a page up in no time.

What people do not realize is that they do not control the content that they post on social media in the same way that they own and control the content on their own website.[1]

It's a complex area but the way I look at it when setting up a page on Facebook, for example, is it's as if I took my lawn chair to a giant Facebook stadium and found a nice spot on the grass. "Hey, I staked it out first, and it sort of feels like mine." Except when Mark Zuckerberg gets on the loudspeaker and announces that it's private property. Oh, and he has some new rules about who can stay and who must leave, or what you can say or do in his stadium.

If you do not have a site because you're camping out on other people's property, you are taking a risk. You should first have your own website, and then by all means use social media to the fullest.

That way, you can keep your very best stuff on your own property and direct any social-media posts ultimately to your site.

Mistake #2: Having a Site That Doesn't Even Do the Minimum

This type of site is more or less a business card or brochure that's posted online. It happens all the time when business owners are dragged into the online world against their will, so they say: "Fine. Stick this up there. Then I can put a big checkmark next to: 'Get site done.'"

We saw this in the *SBR* series (and with many business owners we have worked with over the years) where some business owners took care to have a nice physical storefront but at the same time either had no site, or it was this ancient thing that a relative created two years ago and no one had the login information to update. Instead of helping their business it turned off prospective customers.

The sad part is that many more people are likely to see that lousy online storefront than they are to walk by the physical store. Even citizens in the town will often check online for store hours, COVID rules, discounts, and so on. If all they see is a dusty, outdated thing—well, that's a type of branding at work.

Related tip: If you're not going to update a site very often, that's bad. If you don't update it often and you have stuff on there that has dates on it, that's doubly bad. For example, the site says: "Come to our Spring Clearance Sale!" when it's now September.

Mistake #3: Not Arranging Things So That Updates Are a Breeze

The reason sites get ancient is that some of them can be a great pain to update. This is where social media has done a great job: if you're a business owner and a water main just burst down the street, you can literally update your social-media page from your mobile phone.

That's how it should be for basic updates to your site. If that's not the case today, then you need to make that happen. In other words, you need to identify someone whose job description includes keeping the website updated; in that case, you use your phone to contact that person about the water main. The other option is to get your site on a platform that is easily updatable.

We have good options for this at Deluxe, and there are many other alternatives as well. It's not necessary or even advisable to try to do massive updates via a mobile device; you just want to eliminate the friction of making quick changes.

On several SBR episodes, we showed business owners how we configured their sites so that any update they made to Instagram would automatically also update their website. That sort of hands-off updating is the best, and it's what you should insist upon, wherever you have your site done.

Related tip: I would strongly advise against having a good friend or family member keep your site updated. Yes, it can theoretically work, but it often can become a disaster. If the site isn't updated, you might notify, cajole, and beg the person to do it. If it still does not get done, it's hard to fire a relative. This is where this sort of informal arrangement may be fine for a hobby site but is unacceptable for a business site. You need clear accountability from someone who takes the job seriously, and whom you can replace if necessary.

Mistake #4: Having an Awful Domain Name

You want your business to be found easily online by visitors and customers. In the physical world, you'd never consider putting up signs pointing in the wrong direction, so don't do that online, either. It happens several ways:

- **The business wants a name that ends in .com but that is taken, so they settle for .net or .io or some other ending.** The fact is that people will remember the .com version because it's so extremely common. Then they'll be searching for you and will land on the site of the business with the .com ending.
- **Other times, people will find that their favorite name is taken, so they create weird spellings.** For example, if you wanted a site called CookiesForKids.com and it was taken, you might think you're clever by taking the name Cookies4Kids.com. Oh, that's taken too? *Hey I'll just take Cookiez4Kidz.com because it's available!*

Now think of the confusion that will cause. Your business will forever be needing to explain weird spelling: "It's 'cookiez' with a 'Z', okay? Plus it's not the word 'for' but instead it's the number '4'. . ."

You need something that's clean, easily spoken, and in a .com ending. It's interesting how Jeff Bezos first wanted his store to be called Cadabra instead of Amazon. He had the good sense to ask around and when some people misheard it as "cadaver," he decided maybe Amazon was better.[2]

Mistake #5: Paying Too Much for a Website

To people who have no interest in learning web programming or how it all works, the process of getting a site up can seem like a huge, daunting task. Some companies are only too happy to gouge you as a result. You can get your domain name (ex: www.yourcompanysname.com) reserved for about 10 bucks a year, but some companies will charge many times that—because most customers don't know better.

Then there is the whole matter of hooking a domain name up to a website, getting "hosting," configuring email, and so on. Many business owners might opt for a root canal instead of learning all of that. They therefore may shrug and pay literally hundreds of dollars per month for a website, when a perfectly serviceable one should cost less than $50 per month. If you're running a business that has a ton of traffic, then it might go a little higher, but not by much.

Mistake #6: Paying Too Little for a Website

You no doubt have seen the ads online that say: "Get a great website for only $5.95 per month!" Some competitors will even go to $3.95, or lower.

Now think about that. How can they possibly be making money and providing a good service for that cost? They can't. If it seems too good to be true, it probably is. They are looking for suckers who are only focused on cost and not on what they get for that cost. What's the catch? Some of these companies will sell advertising space on your site! Others will give you a terrible domain name that starts with their name and ends in yours. So if they are ABCHosting and you are Acme Plumbing, then it will be AcmePlumbing.ABCHosting.com.

Still other shady companies will inform you that you don't own the domain name you registered through them. If you want to leave, it's going to cost you big bucks to buy it off them. Hey, it was all in the 50-page fine-print agreement you signed two years ago. The world may be changing at breakneck speed, but that old saying is just as true as ever: you get what you pay for.

Mistake #7: Your Site Is Broken, as Far as Many Visitors Are Concerned

Websites are just a stream of instructions; what actually turns that alphabet soup of numbers and letters into your pretty website is the web browser. That's what you have on your desktop, tablet, and phone. Popular ones are Chrome, Firefox, and Safari, but some people prefer many other browsers.

The problem is that no one regulates how a browser must do its job. Apple has its opinion for Safari, and so does Google for Chrome. Therefore, while one browser may display your site just as you intended for it to appear, another browser may have images that cover part of the text, or big blank spots on the pages.

If you're not into these types of details, then you'll need someone to check how your site looks on different browsers. You can actually do this for free in Google Chrome. It's beyond the scope of this book to go into the details, but it's trivial for someone to do who's competent enough to build your site. It should be done at no extra cost.

Mistake #8: Your Site Looks Awful on Mobile Devices

It's possible that you avoid Mistake #7 and everything is in its proper place when looking at your web pages. The only problem is that many sites do not bother to adapt the pages to be viewed on a screen that is a couple of inches across.

You've seen this many times: the site is a full page of text that's been squashed to postage-stamp size, so the text is completely unreadably small. You have to pinch and pinch to get it large enough to read. Then you have to scroll to the left and right to see parts of the page.

It's infuriating and unnecessary. What you want is what's called a "responsive site" for mobile users. That's where the page width is much narrower and longer, and the text is larger. It's much more pleasant to view a site on a mobile device this way.

This is not just an aesthetic preference: more people now view websites on mobile devices than they do on desktops or tablets. Google has said that its primary focus is on how websites look on mobile devices. In other words, if you don't create a good visitor experience on mobile, Google will ding your site and rank it lower.

Mistake #9: Your Site Looks Okay, But It Takes Forever to Appear After Someone Types in Your Address

This is both a common problem and a serious one. Think about your own behavior: if a site is slow to load, after just a few seconds you most likely give up and go elsewhere. So do I. Sure, if I *must* visit the site because it's the Internal Revenue Service and I need to submit a form, then I may not have a choice. But people have lots of choices when it comes to small businesses, and little patience for slow-loading sites. They will shop elsewhere at the drop of a hat.

You can see how fast your site loads from Google's perspective if you google "Google PageSpeed Insights." It's a free tool that has lots of technical detail for your web person, but it also has an overall score for you to see.

Mistake #10: You Have Typical Stock Images on Your Site

"Stock photography" refers to when you buy an image from a company to use on your site. You should never just grab an image from some site and stick that image on your website. That is a good way to get sued, or at the very least to be forced to pay a lot of money for your use of that image. The Internet has become very sophisticated about finding images that are used without authorization.[3] It's called "photo infringement" and you'll pay the price if you do that.

That's why stock-photo agencies exist, where they're happy to sell you images for use on your site for a few bucks. The only problem is that many of the images look very artificial and contrived. We've all seen the shots of some guy in a suit, with a briefcase in hand, jumping over hurdles. It may have been clever at one point, but now it just looks tired and fake.

I don't know anything about your business, but I can confidently advise you to stay away from cheesy, fake, or gimmicky stuff. We live in an age where anything at all can be created by computer and shown on the movie screen. People generally prefer authenticity over fake, artificial stuff. Especially after COVID, authenticity is essential.

This is all to say that you're better off not paying for images from a stock agency and simply shooting some photographs yourself. Have a friend shoot them if you don't want to do it. People can detect fake stuff from a mile away, so you'll save money and be more effective at the same time.

This is a key element Deluxe has advised businesses on and provided to those selected for *SBR*. Photos of your own goods, services, and location are essential and so much better than stock photography. When we build websites for *SBR* businesses, we always insist on having professional photographs taken to show off the business. If you can't afford to do that yourself, even high-quality photos from your phone will work better than artificial stock images. And, yes, your phone actually is quite a capable camera.

Mistake #11: You Don't Get to the Point Quickly

People are short on time. Not only do they leave if a site loads slowly, but they leave if the site has a bunch of baloney up front, in the form of stock images and text that does not get to the point quickly. I think this often happens because a business owner sometimes gets enamored with their site as a piece of art or a creative expression of their personality. Maybe, but that is crazy thinking. The purpose of the website is to drive sales. If it's a work of modern art that doesn't sell anything, you failed.

In Chapter 7 we talk about how to get people's attention and persuade them to act. It's even more important when your customer is waiting in some line, looking at her phone, and is on your site. You have mere seconds to convince her to keep scrolling down. Use those seconds wisely. Look at your site using your mobile device and see if the first bit that loads is something that tells your story engagingly. If not, adjust the text and images until it does justice to your business.

Mistake #12: Your Site Does Not Include Links to "Terms of Service" and "Privacy Policy" Pages

Let me say right up front that this stuff bores me to tears. If I were an insomniac, all I'd need to do is read a website's terms of service, and I'd sleep like a baby.

Even so, you need the disclosure. If you go to any reputable business and scroll to the very bottom of their homepage, you'll see links to "terms of service" and "privacy policy." As boring as this language is, it's necessary because the Internet has evolved to the point that governmental authorities expect certain information on your site. If you don't have it, you can hope that they won't notice—and hope is not a strategy. Part of being the real deal is having boring stuff like these documents. By the way, Google also expects to see these basic disclosures. If you do not have them, Google will rank your site lower.

Please note: It's not a good idea to rip off someone else's privacy policy and terms of service and put them on your site. Not only might they sue you for copyright infringement if the words match too closely, but it may not adequately protect you. Part of the cost of doing business is to pay an attorney to have these documents customized to your business. Consider it to be a form of online insurance.

Mistake #13: You Don't Have Your Site Backed Up

It's a good thing that the Internet operates invisibly, because if it did not, you'd be shocked. Hackers with very little experience can buy programs that run 24/7, looking for websites that are easy targets.

Once they find a site that matches their criteria, they try to guess the login password. Their automated systems try literally thousands of the obvious ones like: "password123" "123456789," "qwerty," "iloveyou," and many more. When they crack the password, they take control of the website, encrypt the data, and post some sort of notice. Then either the owner notices the break-in, or a customer brings it to their attention.

Now it's going to cost thousands of dollars to agree to the hacker's terms. In the case of hospitals and whole cities that have fallen victim to ransomware, the price can run into the six figures or more.[4]

Deluxe hosts millions of websites for clients, and this is one of the first things we tell businesses: back up your files. If you're hacked, you may not be able to meet the hackers' ransom demands and your files may be gone forever. Rebuilding everything from scratch is an expensive nightmare. Actually, having multiple backups, on multiple separate, unlinked devices is savvy. This way the bad actors would have to hack multiple systems to harm your business, making someone else's business an easier target.

If hacked businesses had spent a fraction of the ransom amount to back up their data, they could have laughed at the ransom demands. That's because they would have the entire site and data backed up in at least one place, and preferably more. If their system had been creating daily backups, then the business owner could have followed a simple process to wipe away the hacked site and revert it to what it looked like yesterday or last month, before the attack.

Mistake #14: You Have Ineffective Passwords and Procedures for Them

As I mentioned earlier, many businesses choose passwords that are comfortable instead of comforting. Comfortable passwords are easy to remember by the owner. Comforting passwords are so long that it would take literally thousands of years for computers to crack them. That's what you want.

Many people think that short passwords are fine if they're made up of random stuff like "78ac#@p9$." That is a difficult password for a human to guess, but it's trivial for a computer to crack, when it tries all combinations of nine characters. You are much better off by creating long passwords using normal words that are easy to type but make no sense. To put it another way, the random password of "78ac#@p9$" is far, far easier to crack than the longer password of "FalconsWinSuper-Bowlin2022."

By the way, don't make the mistake of thinking that you're too small for the bad actors to take notice. As I said earlier, they have systems that run 24/7 until they find a victim, and the criminal activity is automated. They're often overseas so they are not concerned about investigations or lawsuits.

As for password procedures, I strongly recommend that you use a password manager like 1Password or LastPass. Then you'll only need to remember one password—to get into that system—and the system will do the rest.

The password manager can create crazy-long passwords that protect you better, but you never have to remember them or type them in. The system takes care of that.

No matter whether you use a password manager or not, you should not use the same username and password combination for multiple important sites. Hackers know that people do this for convenience, so once they've hacked you in one place, they simply turn on an automated tool that tries that same combination in thousands of other places.

And finally, do not share your passwords with others. Yes, they're trusted friends or family, but sometimes their systems will get hacked and when they log into something using your password, their compromised computer can spread to your systems. It's better to compartmentalize.

Mistake #15: You Do Not Keep Your Website or Computer Updated

This advice may seem eye-rollingly obvious, but it is one of the main ways businesses get hacked. It happens again and again: somebody identifies a weakness in some software that businesses use. The software company issues a patch to fix the problem. Now, human nature takes over, because a small percentage of businesses are on the ball and patch their systems right away. A large percentage of the remainder take their sweet time. There is no shortage of excuses for not patching it now:

- "I'll get around to it soon."
- "It's on my 'to do' list."
- "I'm in the middle of a project."
- "I'll have Rashid take care of it when he's back from vacation."

These excuses are absolute music to the ears of hackers. Why? Because they were just handed a roadmap!

The software company announced there is a software problem—and sometimes it's an extremely serious vulnerability. Now the hackers simply need to look for websites and computers that have not been patched. It's as if the mayor of a town announced: "Attention Centerville citizens! One of our stores downtown is unlocked and unattended. All police are dealing with an issue in the neighboring town." Most people would do nothing, but a small number would drop what they were doing and clean out the unattended store.

Patching is free and quick to implement. It's every bit as important as locking the door to your business.

Mistake #16: You Don't Have an Online Form on Your Site, But Instead Rely on People Contacting You Through Your Email Address

At any given time, a large number of people are having problems with their email systems. If email is the only way they can contact you from your site, you'll miss out on some business. In addition, putting your email address on your site is an invitation to be spammed to death by systems that grab or "scrape" emails from sites automatically and sell them to spammers.

It's much better to have a form on your site where people can enter their information and hit "Send" or "Submit." It does not rely on their own email system, and you can be instantly notified of their message. This kind of contact form is trivial for your web person to set up and it should not cost you anything extra.

You can have multiple forms for different purposes: one to sign up to be notified of sales, one for subscribing to your newsletter, and so on.

~~~

If you read through these 16 mistakes and you have not been making them, that's impressive! If some of them apply to you, then it's your lucky day, because all of the fixes are relatively easy, and many of them cost little to nothing.

Now let's get into some territory that few small businesses take full advantage of. Sometimes online-marketing people can be about as bad as the military for coining acronyms for everything. In the online world you may have come across terms like SEO, SEM, PPC, CPM, CRM, SERP, and many more. Let's speak some plain English here, shall we? The two areas I want to discuss now are "organic search" and "paid search."

Two Big Visibility Boosters

Visibility Booster #1: Organic Search

Part of me thinks: *Maybe I should skip talking about search altogether; after all, lots of people know about it already.* Then I recall the many *SBR* episodes in which businesses didn't even have websites, never mind using them effectively to get found by people online.

Think about that. More than 20 years after the World Wide Web was created, some businesses still don't have websites. In Season 1, we met Matt Haynes, a former pastor who opened Filament Tattoo in Wabash, Indiana. Now a pastor who owns a tattoo parlor is a great story unto itself, but few businesses lend themselves to the idea of a visual website the way a tattoo parlor can. Being able to showcase the work and artistry of his team was paramount, yet in 2016, Matt lacked a website. We fixed that. We've done the same in every season since then!

My goal here is not to give you a full briefing on organic search, because you can read some other book for that. Instead, I'll again invoke the 80/20 Rule and give you the key activities you should consider having done for your business. I say "having done" because you may be able to do some of the activities yourself, and you'll probably delegate others.

This term "organic search" is fitting because the activity refers to the things that you build and grow from the ground up, organically, versus buying them ready-made. When it's done right, it can mean a steady flow of visitors to your site and customers to your business.

The Great Matchmaker. Think of the whole concept of search as one big matchmaking service, with Google being "Matchmaker-in-Chief." There are plenty of other search engines besides Google, but they pale in size by comparison. For that matter, the second-largest search engine in the world is YouTube, and Google owns it, too.

On the one hand, you have billions of people searching for things. Though it's true that countless hours are spent by people chatting online, yelling at each other on Twitter, and trading funny-cat videos, even so, search has transformed our lives. Now when we get sick, we're able to read all about various symptoms before talking with a doctor. If the water heater is failing, we can do thorough research on new water heaters, and on the plumbers to install one.

So here you have customers searching for water heaters and plumbers; you have plumbers searching for customers; and you have water-heater manufacturers, who want to be attractive to both plumbers and customers. All of this happens in an extremely noisy environment filled with all those cat videos, sports scores, angry Tweets, and whatnot.

Google has put an enormous amount of time and money into the issue of how to create the best matches for all concerned. Their formula or algorithm contains hundreds of "signals" of what they look for in a good site and by one estimate, they make changes to the algorithm 500 to 600 times per year.[5] Oh, and the exact details are secret, so people aren't able to force their websites to the top.

Google is all about "search intent." When someone types into Google the word "iPhone," what does that person want to see? It may at first seem obvious, but there could be many different intents:

- What is an iPhone?
- Current cost of iPhones
- Latest iPhone models
- iPhone reviews
- History of the iPhone for a term paper

These are just a few. Google is continuously "crawling" or analyzing all the websites it can find online, and its computers try to figure out the themes of those sites. Then they try to match the intent of the person searching with the intent or theme of a particular website.

Although Google at one level is secretive about the algorithm, they do make it clear that some website characteristics are desirable. In other words, they'll rank your website higher in the search-results pages (the SERPs) better if you have them. Here are some of the larger factors:

- **Google loves to see "authoritative" content.** If Site A has a paragraph comparing electric lawnmowers, and Site B has separate whole pages with good details on each electric lawnmower, then Google will favor Site B.
- **Sites that do not have terms of service and privacy policies are downgraded**, as I mentioned before.
- **Websites that load very slowly will be downgraded**, as I also mentioned earlier.
- **Google measures visitor engagement.** If people type in "heirloom tomato seeds" and Google sends them to your page all about those seeds, Google times how long those people stay on that page. If they arrive and immediately leave, that's called a "bounce." Visitors must not have found the site interesting or maybe the page was broken. Then again, if they find your material engaging and stick around, Google figures that's a great sign that this site should rank highly in the SERPs for "heirloom tomato seeds" and they'll maybe even rank you higher in the future.

The thing about the engagement concept is that it differs by what you're trying to accomplish with your site. If you sell to engineers, then high engagement might be due to lots of details, specifications, and research on the page. If you're marketing to cat lovers, then high engagement will likely involve photos or videos of interesting kitties.

Therefore, the sites that rank best in Google are ones that do not try to be all things to all people. **Google likes crisp distinctions.** Therefore, do not create one page with tons of different products and services on it. You'll be ranked higher by Google if you have separate pages that each has a distinct theme.

We visited Keystone Boxing in Season 2, Episode 6. Jose Tilapa, the owner, can do a lot of things. Instead of creating one web page with all of them listed, Jose will be much better served by having separate pages for his kids' program, the fitness classes, and the professional boxing coaching.

You know this is true as a customer. When you're on the hunt for "Japanese hand-forged kitchen knives" you're delighted if you see a page all about exactly that. You're disappointed if you find a page that has pocketknives, hunting knives, and oh yes, one Japanese kitchen knife.

It's fine to have your homepage be a summary of everything you offer. However, wherever possible, also have separate pages for all the interesting different products or services you want to be known for.

Google loves fresh content, because people love fresh content. You are much better off by updating your site a little bit and regularly, instead of doing one big push to renovate your site—and then have it remain static for months.

One way to do this is to create a blog, where you can quickly post some thoughts on a new product you're reviewing or takeaways from a Zoom expo you attended. With a blog, you don't need to post lengthy, authoritative treatments of a topic, but you should be regularly contributing to it. The most successful bloggers—in other words, the most visible bloggers on Google—will establish a cadence of posting daily or weekly and then will make a point of sticking to that cadence.

I try to post weekly about Deluxe.

Fresh content was even more important during the pandemic of 2020. Businesses that were trying to reach customers for online or takeout orders had to create fresh content to help customers fully understand how to support or interact with the business. Yet we all witnessed some businesses fail to adapt and notify their customers, even with the life of the business at stake.

Compliance Is Mandatory. The "Americans with Disabilities Act" (ADA) is a big deal. As the Internet has become more sophisticated, it's begun to get better at meeting the needs of all visitors, including ones with disabilities.

Think about images on your site. How can Google—which is essentially a computer—know what your image of a lovely sunset scene is about? It's starting to change, but for now, you need to tell Google what the image contains. You do this by telling your website person to use "alt tags" for all images. It's now a requirement in order to be compliant with ADA rules. By the way, businesses with websites that do not follow certain accessibility guidelines run the risk of getting sued.[6]

You should also tell your web person to fill in the "metadata" for each page. This information is what you tell the Google computers to show on the search results page when Google displays what your page is about. It's only a suggestion to Google, which can decide to show something else, but it's useful to have all the same.

Google Is Crucial for Business Visibility. When you type the name of a business into Google, you'll usually see a bunch of information displayed on the right side of the search-results page. It will show photos of the business, plus its address, hours of operation, phone number, and many other details.

You should be all over that section of the page. You want it to display your site and business in the best light. You can do that by going to https://www.google.com/business/ and filling out the details of your business.

Google makes it easy for you to manage a page that describes a lot about your business. Take full advantage of it. You should provide whatever information they ask for. And if that information changes, make it a priority to update Google. For example, if your operating hours changed during COVID, you should have updated Google. If you have new photographs after a renovation, go in there and upload the photos.

As I said elsewhere and we saw in several *SBR* episodes, businesses are leaving piles of money on the table if they do not take full advantage of Google categories. These are tags or designators that help Google to classify your business properly.

It's actually a little complicated, when you consider how many different types of businesses are out there. Also, if you're a hotel, you may wonder if you can be classified under a bunch of categories like lodging, restaurant, golf, spa, and so on. Some businesses go crazy with the categories, and try to claim that they're too many different things. Google says that the best way to choose is to select categories that complete the statement: "this business IS a _____" rather than "this business HAS a ____."[7] It's worth the time to get this right, because it has the potential to bring you immediate business at zero cost to you.

Be warned, though: Google's computer robots sometimes will make decisions for you about what your business is, your hours of operation, whether you're wheelchair-accessible, and so on—and Google sometimes is wrong. They'll even sometimes get your business name wrong. You should put a note in your calendar to check your "Google My Business" listing regularly, to make sure a robot didn't do an update and misrepresent your business.[8]

The bottom line is that Google is the biggest of big dogs. It's a high-payoff activity for you or someone you designate to continuously keep Google updated on the details of your business, and monitor that Google got it right. Don't just tweet out your new hours or tell Facebook about them; make sure Google knows the current details, too. You'll be rewarded with a prominent online business-building presence.

I hear from many business owners that they just "don't want to mess with all that social-media stuff." That is a huge mistake. You *must* get comfortable with the reality of social media today, or likely perish at some point in the future.

Reviews Can Make or Break You. It used to be that if a business treated its customers badly, very few people would know about it at the time. Perhaps word would eventually get around, but for the most part, only the business had the full picture of customer complaints.

Those days died with the phone booth. Now customers can leave reviews on Google, Yelp, TripAdvisor, and dozens of other review sites.

The reviews are pretty much available in real time, businesses cannot edit them, and some can go on for hundreds of words.

Of course, on the flipside, when your business does a great job, these reviews are worth their cyberweight in gold. The social proof of dozens or hundreds of nonpaid strangers raving about your business is one of the most powerful tools you could ever have for getting more business.

Just as I said that you must make it a priority to keep Google updated on the details of your business and monitor that they got it right, you must continually monitor your reviews. If you don't, your business can suffer.

If someone runs a business that delivers lousy service, then eventually reviews will reflect that. In a sense it's simply online justice.

But what about when you run a business where you try hard to please customers, and some customers are simply unreasonable? Some will leave blazingly bad reviews. Oh, and what about your competitors? Some of them may ask a friend or second cousin to leave you a terrible review, just to drag down your online reputation.

The thing **not** to do is to ignore these negative reviews. You may be the type of person who wants to focus on the positive. Some of the bad reviews may be justified, but you shrug and think: *Hey, no one's perfect.* You may also figure that some of the bad reviews are indeed fabricated and there's no use trying to correct the record.

You would be wrong. Most new potential customers—the very people you're trying to attract—start with a blank slate. They don't know you, and they are about to make a very fast judgment about whether to go with you, or just move their finger or mouse and click to a competitor.

Let's say you sell a product on Amazon. It's a metal firepit for people to enjoy in their backyards. There are three types of negative reviews you might get.

Justified negative reviews. The customer might say that your product arrived with no instructions, and it was a real pain to figure out which way was up for some of the parts. This sort of review rings true, because it's so specific. Shoppers will read this one, and then see if other people have the same complaint. If they do, then the shopper judges it as valid.

Now it could be that some customers buy from you anyway, because they're handy with tools and are confident that they're smarter than these reviewers. Maybe so. But you also want buyers who are not so handy with tools, don't you? The best thing for you to do is respond to each of those justified negative reviews.

Hello, thanks for leaving your review. We can see your point that we didn't include specific instructions for assembling that firepit. That's our mistake and we apologize. We will correct this problem in future shipments, and for the time being, you can go to our site (Amazon doesn't allow us to put a link here) and type in "firepit assembly instructions" and you'll have them right away. Again, sorry for the inconvenience and thanks for your business!

Now what do you suppose shoppers will think about that? *Wow, the company actually responded and took responsibility. I like that. It's rare. Maybe I'll consider them after all.*

It is easy to want to defend yourself and your business. But understanding the customer's point of view gives you an opportunity to retain that customer and attract more with the right response.

Unwarranted negative reviews. These can really get under your skin because they're not justified, and you might think, *What an idiot this customer is.* You may even be right. You may offer an iron firepit and a stainless steel one. You said in plain English on the Amazon page that the iron firepit *will rust if it is not covered*, but it's a fabulous value for what you get. You suggest in the description that they cover the pit when not in use. Then you see reviewers going on about how the firepit rusted. In this case, you might say:

Hello, thanks for leaving your review. We're sorry that you are disappointed that the iron firepit rusted. We try our best to be very conspicuous in our description that it is our iron firepit, and not our stainless steel one. We suggested that people keep the iron one covered. However, we recognize that sometimes rust can happen very quickly. Our firepits are heavy duty, so you should be able to take some steel wool or a rust cleaner like CLR and your pit will look like new again. Thanks for your business.

What do you suppose shoppers will conclude? Probably something like, *Well, what did the dumb customer think would happen with iron? Some people. At least the company was polite and helpful.*

Vague negative reviews. These tend to be the one-star reviews when the vast majority of people are giving much higher ratings. These people will say things like "It sucks" or "Don't buy." They are so vague as to be unlikely to change anyone's minds about your product.

If there is a category to ignore, it would be this one. Then again, you could leave a short reply like: "Hey, sorry you didn't like it. If it is something specific, please call our support line during business hours and we'll be happy to see what we can do." Any shopper reading this exchange will think, *Another lazy, vague reviewer. Probably a competitor. It was a good reply from the company, though.*

Of course, your competitors will not bother to be so careful to follow up with negative reviews, and you'll look good by comparison.

One note: You should not limit your reviews to people who leave negative comments. If you do that, then the people who took the time to leave positive comments may think, *Hey what about me?*

Reinforce that positive behavior! Thank the positive reviewers, and you'll stand out that much more from your competition.

Visibility Booster #2: Paid Search

When you hear terms like "paid search," "search engine marketing," and "pay per click," they all pretty much mean the same thing: you pay for instant visibility.

The organic search we just finished talking about is something you grow over time. You are not directly paying someone for visibility. Instead, you may pay someone to do social-media posts, or write articles, and these in turn generate visibility.

Lots of paid-search sites will be happy to take your money, like Google, Microsoft Ads, Facebook, and so on. There are quite a few similarities between them, and you know by now that I'm not doing a full tutorial on each concept I mention in this book. So you have the big picture about paid search; here are the main moving parts. I'll use an example of how a local building contractor could use it with a service called Google Ads.

1. **You decide what terms or "keywords" you want to be found for.** With literally billions of people online, it's impossible to be visible everywhere instantly, unless perhaps you'll be the first person to travel to Mars.

   After you thought in Chapter 2 about your most-profitable products, you decided that you'd love more sales of wooden decks. In other words, when someone searches for "wood deck," "wooden deck," or "deck contractor," you want your business to show up.

2. **You decide where you want your ads shown.** You don't want to pay for visibility in LA when you build decks around Dallas. You can tell the system to only show your ads to people in Dallas, or in certain ZIP codes, or even within a 25-mile radius of your office, among other options.

3. **You decide how much you're willing to pay for this visibility.** You can limit your budget to $10 per day if you wish, or you could say "I want to show up as #1 in the search results if anyone types 'deck contractor' within 10 miles of my office."

4. **You create little ads that either have just a few lines of text or include images.** Any time the above conditions are met, Google will show your ad.

5. **If people click on your ad, you need to decide where they should be taken.** You might think: *Duh, how about taking them to my website homepage?*

That's usually a mistake, and here's why: Remember how I said earlier that Google likes specialization, and so do customers? Most homepages of websites are general. If I'm a building contractor, my homepage will mention that we build houses, replace roofs, have a wide selection of siding, build decks, and provide several other services. Yet if I want a deck, I want a specialist who's great at decks, and I have no interest in roofs at the moment. Therefore, it's best to take people right to a page on your site that's all about decks.

The actual system has many sophisticated elements, and I've merely done an overview here, but still, you have the big picture: you pay, and Google will deliver people in your area searching for "deck contractors" to the page you specify. And you only pay Google if someone actually clicks on your ad. Pretty cool, huh?

So why doesn't everyone just do paid search and be done with marketing? The main reason is that Google auctions off the visibility. In effect, it says: "Who is willing to pay the most for the top spot on this page?" If you have few competitors for some super-narrow product, then the price may be a few cents every time someone clicks on your ad. Then again, if you're an attorney specializing in getting people out of jail, you may literally pay 58 *dollars* every time someone types in "bail bonds" and clicks on your ad.[9] It's that competitive a term.

I don't want to scare you off; I simply want to give you the perspective that paid search can be amazingly useful if you learn more about it or have someone else learn it. Then you can start with only a few dollars per day and measure the results. If you know your numbers the way we talked about in Chapter 2, then you can pay a few dollars to bring very specifically targeted people—your target market—to your site.

Now you have one more arrow in your quiver—one more capability that separates you from most competitors.

~~~

We've covered a lot of material that will get you very well prepared to grow your business. In the next chapter, we discuss specific methods of bringing in that business.

6

Bringing in Business

You Can Have the best brand in terms of what you want to be known for, but if almost no one knows about you in the first place, then you have a more fundamental problem.

It's as if you created a wonderful image but it's on a postage stamp on the side of the road. At the same time, a competitor has this fuzzy blob of a brand, but it's on a billboard by the highway. You need both the brand quality and the visibility to succeed.

Where can people find you? Of course, if you have a physical storefront, then some people will notice you when passing by. Then again, we saw in Season 4, Episode 6 that Zion Climbing Center had no sign (that is, if you ignore the spray-painted graffiti sign on a wall outside). The nonprofit was run on a shoestring and that's commendable, but if would-be customers or even donors drive by and don't know about it, that's a problem.

A Chiropractor's Secret

There was a chiropractor who became wealthy after being able to open many offices. He had a pattern of setting up an office in a new town, and before long he was able to build that business to be the largest in town.

After a while he was invited to be on a panel discussion at a chiropractic conference where there was a session about business building. Someone in the audience said: "I've heard that you are able to get as many as 80 customers in a month. That's unbelievably good. What method do you use to get 80 customers?" The chiropractor said: "I don't have a method that generates 80 customers. The truth is I have about 80 methods that each brings in one or two customers a month—and I do them all."

You should take some time now and write down every way that—to your knowledge—people today discover that you exist. No doubt there's word of mouth; maybe you advertise locally; and so on. After you create that list, you can compare it with the many methods we'll now cover.

One common theme in *SBR* episodes and also with the small businesses that contact our call centers is that when asked how customers find them, invariably the answer is word of mouth. That's an important channel, for sure. But to grow your business, you need many more channels. Marketing your business is as important as having a business plan or maintaining inventory.

Community-Based Business-Building Methods

Working with other businesses to co-promote. Ellen's Bridal & Dress Boutique was a great example of this in Episode 3 of Season 1. After all, when a bride-to-be is shopping for everything that's needed for a wedding, it may involve the dress, flowers, shoes, jewelry, a cake, the venue, photography, a limo—the list goes on. The businesses that provide these products and services do not compete with each other, but they sure can help each other. Lisa Ellen Downs offered the dresses, and she got together with several other businesses in Wabash to offer a bridal expo. Talk about a win/win: the brides-to-be save time by seeing many vendors in one place, and each business gets exposure to many potential customers at once. Lisa spent $200 on the event and sold 20 dresses.

Even apart from doing an expo, this kind of collaboration makes a ton of sense for each participating business. If someone books a limo for a wedding, it's so easy for the limo company to have materials on hand to mention the other businesses to that customer.

This same kind of collaboration works in many situations. A real estate agent becomes aware of someone moving into town and could refer a plumber, electrician, attorney, dog-walking service, you name it. The local hospital of course knows when babies are born, and can have materials from florists, traveling nurses, massage therapists, and so on.

Bulletin boards. This method has been around forever, and it's still a good one. Whether you have a physical or online product or service, there are places with bulletin boards around town and in surrounding towns. They may be in barber shops, bus or train stations, the local YMCA, a diner, or many other locations. Sometimes people have time on their hands while waiting for transportation or to be seated to eat. Even though lots of people revert to looking at their mobile phones at such times, not everyone does.

Signs around town. You've no doubt seen signs for "We Buy Houses" or weight-loss solutions posted up on telephone poles. This may not be the most elegant way to advertise, but if it meets town ordinances, it can be effective. People having nothing to do at a stop sign will get a little brand injection this way from an enterprising business.

Business cards around town. The most legendary example of using this method is Joe Girard. He stuttered until the age of 35 because his father had continually put him down. Joe got therapy, fixed his stuttering, and got into sales. He became listed in the *Guinness Book of World Records* for selling the most cars in a year.[1]

One of Joe's favorite selling tools was his business card. He'd put several into the glove compartment of each new car, with the customer's name written on the back. He explained to the car's owner that if those cards came back to him, the customer would get a reward. Joe did stuff like bring a bag of the cards to football games and throw them out by the handful in the stadium.

Although that may not be your style, you should seriously consider how to up your business-card game. First, make sure you use both sides of the card. The entire back and some of the front should be devoted to your brand and why people should work with you.

Second, make the card memorable. You can accomplish that with a photo, or the color of the card, or the typeface. It might not even be a standard card, but could be a double card that folds to standard size, or crazy-but-effective things like casino chips.

Of course, much depends on the business you run, but the point is there is no limit to the creativity some people have brought to business cards. At Deluxe, we offer promotional products like business cards. Our sales reps talk with creative businesses all day and can give you ideas about unique cards. Think about the business cards you have decided to keep. Look them over and figure out why. You'll get at least a few ideas that way.

Just as some salespeople have quotas for how many calls they make each day, some successful people have a goal for how many cards they give out. When you get creative about it, pretty soon you realize that you can accidentally leave your card at the gas pump when you fill up, or in the home center near the "For Sale" signs that homeowners buy. Turn it into a game.

Joe Girard would mail his business card every month to people who hadn't bought a car (yet) but had kicked the tires, so to speak. He'd write a note on each card each month. January was "Happy New Year," February was "Happy Valentine's Day," and so on. Most car salespeople cannot be bothered to send one card to the customers who bought! Joe sent monthly cards to prospects. Now when the time came for those prospects to buy a car, who do you suppose was on the top of their minds?

Becoming a donor or sponsor for something. Every town has sports leagues for kids, charities, organizations like Kiwanis, Shriners, American Legion, Scouts, and churches. All these entities are pretty much in full fund-raising mode all the time for the good work they do. They're the glue that keeps cities and towns together in somewhat the same way that small businesses do.

When you donate time, money, or materials to these places, they're grateful and will sometimes give the business a little ad space in a publication as thanks. That may not be the time to talk up your upcoming whiskey-tasting event, but it's yet another way to get visibility.

Through *SBR* we met Brian Weavel, owner of Anna's Pizza and Pasta in Winnebago, Illinois. Brian became a fan of the show and, like any good small-business owner, he used numerous marketing tools to reach customers. Brian was extremely active on social media and posted constantly about his business, his community, and his love of SBR. But where Brian truly succeeded was in his ability to be a community cheerleader through his business. He made a point of sponsoring high school and youth sports teams, furthering his brand but also being a good community partner.

Though Brian has closed Anna's Pizza and Pasta and moved on to a new career path, he was adamant throughout the pandemic that the community and businesses support each other. As he pointed out, the small-business community was always there with a sponsorship dollar. Now, during an unprecedented time, giving back to those businesses was essential.

Chamber of Commerce listing. If you're part of the Chamber of Commerce or the local downtown association, those organizations always have mechanisms to give their members some visibility. You should connect with other members and see about creating the co-promotion arrangement that I mentioned earlier in this chapter.

Other Physical Business-Building Methods

Your customers as ambassadors. No advertising under the sun is quite as effective as satisfied customers telling their friends about you. As consumers, over time we build a list of trusted vendors like doctors, dentists, plumbers, electricians, car-repair people, accountants, and so on. But those vendors retire, move away, or sometimes go bad. That means that at any given time we're in the market for one supplier or another. When a friend says, "You won't believe the experience I had . . ."—and when that experience was mind-blowingly positive—now you have some amazing advertising going on.

We talk more about this in Chapter 8 on relationships, but my point here is that you should have a mechanism for recording when customers refer people to you. You should always ask a new customer or a new prospect: "How did you hear about us?"; you can do that both online and in person. Then think of creative ways to thank the person who referred them to you. In some circumstances, cold hard cash works great! In others, it might be a thank-you note, or a discount or gift to the referrer. It might even be that you refer people to that referrer's own business. Just don't be silent when someone refers you, and that person will become the gift that keeps on giving.

Social media is one of the most-used methods today of sharing how you feel about a business. Deluxe has a product called Reviews Promoter, where it allows a business owner to prompt a customer to write a review. Rather than always asking each customer, a simple text prompt reminds the customer to share their experience. If you make things easy for customers, they're usually happy to respond.

Billboards. Many billboards have been taken down, but that means that the surviving ones have probably been judged to be effective in bringing in business. Many of those are now digital, and the billboard companies may be able to pass on the savings, compared to the old days when they needed a crew to paste up giant sheets of printed paper.

Flyers. As outdated as it may seem to be printing flyers and distributing them manually, consider this: Is it outdated, or is it now an underused method with almost no competition? This form of advertising is dirt cheap when you consider that you have both sides of a piece of letter-size paper to work with. Then again, you could make a flyer be postcard size.

Some businesses have had great success putting flyers under windshield wipers at sporting events, festivals, or concerts; but always put them on the driver's side, so they're easy to reach. Another way to distribute them is to other businesses, in exchange for your displaying their flyers. They could be on a large bulletin board, or near the cash register, or in a waiting area—wherever there is a combination of space and visibility.

Another great way to distribute flyers is as an insert to the local newspaper. If you've ever done any newspaper advertising, you know they charge by the "column inch." That's one inch of text, filling one column on a page. It can be surprisingly expensive. If you ask the newspaper what the cost of doing an insert is, you'll most likely be blown away. You print up the letter-size flyers, and get to use both sides. You deliver them to the newspaper and they mechanically insert them when folding up the edition. You get vastly more space and exposure for what often is quite a low rate.

Is there a diner in your town? If so, here's a tested and proven win/win: businesses get together to print paper placemats, which they provide to the diner for free. This saves the diner money, and all the customers will read the placemat ads while waiting for food. This is a form of old-school advertising that everyone may actually like, when compared with the avalanche of digital messages coming down on us continuously.

By the way, this can even be a small profit center for you. You could offer to be the business that does all the work, and you just ask the other businesses to provide their ads for a few bucks. You collect that money, and insert your own ad while you're at it. This whole process could be delegated to someone, once it's up and running.

Sending postcards or letters. This may seem so "yesterday" when we're all immersed in Internet ads these days, but they remain incredibly effective. And that's exactly the reason why you should consider this marketing method. The amount of direct mail we receive has dropped with the advent of digital advertising. Just take a look at the size of your phone book compared with the old days—if you even still get a phone book at all.

What this means is that you are competing with fewer mail pieces in the mailbox. In addition, most of those other pieces are from huge companies selling insurance and replacement windows. People will sit up and take notice if it's a piece from a local business, especially if it gives them a good reason to look you up. This is a service Deluxe provides to our clients and something that we work closely with our banking clients to create. Targeted marketing campaigns can be extremely effective when they're designed to reach exactly the right customer.

Paid ads online. As we discussed in Chapter 5, you really need to know something about this option as a business owner. You can run ads in Google, Facebook, LinkedIn, YouTube, and a great many other places. Don't conclude that there's no way you can afford to advertise like this, because your cost could be $10 per day if you want.

Newspaper ads. Have you noticed how your local newspaper— and even the major metropolitan ones—are running way fewer pages these days? It's not because less is going on in your community. For the most part, it's mainly because fewer businesses are advertising. If you checked on advertising rates years ago and were put off by how high they were, you may now be pleasantly surprised. Newspapers need ad revenue in the worst way, so they may give you some great rates.

When you contact them, be sure to ask about "remnant space." This is where you do not insist that your ad runs on a particular day, but you're cool about waiting until they have space. On a day when they have a bit of extra space to fill, they'll run your ad. You benefit by getting a significantly lower rate.

Ad costs may be higher in places like larger, metropolitan newspapers, but in community newspapers, they are remarkably affordable. Many suburban communities or small towns still have these types of weekly newspapers that can support the type of local advertising that can benefit your business.

No matter when your ad runs, it will be like what we discussed earlier with direct mail: you'll stand out more because there are fewer competing ads.

If you happen to have a clientele that was not born with a mobile phone in hand, then there's an additional benefit. People who have been accustomed to reading newspapers for many years may prefer that method of seeing ads, versus online. Some highly sophisticated national advertisers recognize this and sell products like space heaters and insurance in local papers around the country.

Paid ads in publications. This is similar to the dynamics of buying space in newspaper ads. Many publications are experiencing lean times in terms of their printed versions. They may be willing to give you comparatively good rates. Besides, as one of a smaller number of total advertisers, you'll get a larger share of attention.

Online Methods

Selling on Craigslist. In my opinion, Craigslist is misunderstood. It started out as a community bulletin board. Then it grew to be quite large and got a reputation as the place you went if you were selling or buying certain services like escorts, massage, and so on. But Craigslist cut that stuff out a few years ago, and now it's back to being a community bulletin board.

It's surprisingly good. You can find good people to hire there, and people who want your products or services. The ads you post are either free or cost literally a few dollars. You can also target them to your local community. Depending on what you have to sell, you can get responses from people on Craigslist within five minutes of your posting something.

Press releases. Though infrequently used, press releases can be another effective tool when done right. The thing is that reporters have certain standards for what they consider to be news. The fact that you cut prices on sausage in your store does not quite rise to the level of media interest.

Then again, if you have some creativity in that DNA of yours, you might get some media attention. Let's say that we're in the midst of a year that the Winter Olympics are being held. Reporters will have covered all the obvious stuff like which athletes are from the local area, which are likely to win gold medals, which athletes overcame a serious injury to make it to the games, and so on. Their job is to write more stories and they're fresh out of ideas.

This is where press releases come to their rescue. Maybe you are a sandwich shop and you do some research. Perhaps a few people from your state are on the Olympic team, and some of them win medals. You could find out what sorts of food they're fond of, and then make a Gold Medal sandwich, plus silver and bronze. As a press release this won't get picked up by the national press, but it may very well be a prominent story in your town's printed and online newspaper. Maybe you are a local brewery, and you are going to provide a special Gold Medal Brew for half price whenever someone wins a medal. Then again, if you sell homeopathic remedies and have a great set of suggestions for sore muscles, the inability to sleep before big events, and so on, you may very well get national press.

Local business listings. We discussed this in Chapter 5, but I want to emphasize its importance. One door closes and another door opens: we've seen the phone book get way smaller, but local online directories have exploded. Google, Yelp, and Facebook all have free pages you can claim for your business. They allow you to describe your business, submit photos, list hours of operation, and display other information. You really should claim the pages by visiting these online services, typing in your business name, and seeing what shows up. They'll each differ slightly in the process of claiming your page, so just follow the directions you see at the time.

If you do not claim your pages, it sends bad signals to the great many people who search online for businesses: it indicates that you are ignorant of how these basic online services work, or you don't care much about being found, or you're out of business.

Responding to reviews. We covered aspects of reviews in Chapter 5, but most businesses are not doing nearly enough here. In the old days, let's say a hardware store didn't treat its customers particularly well. It's possible that customers might conclude that the bad service was an unusual event; maybe the salesperson had a bad day. Even more importantly, the business owner was not highly motivated to do anything about it. He might receive the occasional letter from a disgruntled customer, but who else knew about the letter? They could get filed away—or thrown away.

These days, there's nowhere to hide. Even if you are a business that never claimed your local listings (see the item before this one), customers are free to go online and tell the world exactly what they think about their recent encounter in your business. The listings then give you a numerical rating that reflects the positive or negative nature of those reviews.

Here is the spectrum of businesses in terms of their awareness and level of proactiveness:

- "Huh? What listings? What reviews?"
- They don't claim their listings and don't respond to reviews, period.
- They claim listings, but don't bother to respond to negative reviews.
- They claim listings, and respond defensively and combatively to negative reviews.
- They claim listings, and are polite in their response to negative reviews. If they can prove that a review is inaccurate, they do so gently. If they cannot disagree with a negative review, they apologize on the spot.
- The best businesses claim listings, handle negative reviews as I just mentioned, and they also thank positive reviewers.

Naturally, only a tiny percentage of businesses respond fully and appropriately. This is yet another opportunity for you to stand out from the crowd.

Your personal listing on LinkedIn. LinkedIn is a little bit of a special situation. It's a type of social media, but it really focuses on businesses. It's not where you take a selfie, the way some other social-media sites encourage. I am always amazed that serious businesspeople post nonprofessional headshots on LinkedIn. This makes them look foolish and unprofessional. Your LinkedIn profile page is your resume for everyone to see.

Hundreds of millions of businesses are on LinkedIn, and it's possible to have both company pages and individual pages. This is my opinion, but the real power of LinkedIn is in the personal page you create as a business owner. This is the place for you to become a "thought leader," as they say, about your business. Maybe you have no interest in that. But if you really are trying to do everything you can to increase your business visibility, you should create a personal page. Then get into the habit of posting small, frequent, useful insights about running the type of business you run.

For example, maybe you are Lena's Pizza, Subs & Wings, which we featured in Season 5, Episode 4. Matt Swank, the owner, was in the corporate world and made the switch to pizzeria owner. Furthermore, he thrived during the COVID mess, given how people wanted to get takeout food.

Matt might think that no one is interested in his story and insights, but he'd be wrong. I've discovered over many years that no matter how successful—or not—you are, there is someone behind you and someone ahead of you.

Therefore, if Matt created a personal page on LinkedIn, he could create lots of posts. They could be on topics like how to keep delivery people safe during COVID; techniques he found effective for sourcing flour and other ingredients during the pandemic; how the business economics changed for him in 2020; a checklist he created in order to decide when to open another store; and so on. There must be thousands of people in the United States and abroad who would be interested in such insights.

There's another use for LinkedIn: if you happen to be a business that sells products or services to other businesses, then you should check out LinkedIn's advertising services. You can create a small ad and target other businesses with an astonishingly precise set of parameters. It could be CEOs of small hotel chains in southwest Indiana, or whatever. Then you only pay LinkedIn when one of those targeted people clicks on your ad and goes to a page you prepare on your website. For a few dollars you can deliver a highly targeted message to a highly targeted audience.

Your website. We spent time in Chapter 5 discussing website mistakes businesses make. I listed the item here again for the sake of having a complete list of online methods.

Answering questions on Quora. This is an unusual service, and it's a child of the online age we now live in. Quora is a place where you can ask questions and have them answered, or you can answer other people's questions.

Please be aware up front that some people on Quora ask dumb questions or junk questions like: "What is the most shocking thing you found in your spouse's possessions?" Then again, you can ask really good questions and get excellent answers. You might ask something arcane like: "I'm the owner of a golf course. I'm looking for a company that rehabilitates golf carts for a reasonable fee. Do you know of anyone?" You may be surprised that someone out of the blue will answer your question with something really useful.

If you spend a little time on Quora, you may find that you can answer other people's questions about the area you're knowledgeable in. Then you'll remember to come back to this service when the shoe is on the other foot, and you need guidance from an expert about some obscure topic.

Upwork or Fiverr. These are online marketplaces to buy or sell services. Elsewhere I've given you more-detailed advice about how to find good vendors, but in this case I'm talking about being one of the vendors.

Take Lighthouse Sounds in Season 3, Episode 7. They could use Upwork or Fiverr and offer to record, edit, and do other professional services for musicians, professional speakers, and celebrities. If you're another type of service-based business, this is a great way to fill slow periods in your calendar, or get your business launched with some of your first clients. It can also provide testimonials and social proof, which is so important in order to grow your business.

Selling on Amazon, eBay, Etsy, and Facebook Marketplace. If you offer physical products, you have a lot of outlets for making additional sales. First there was eBay, and it's still a lively marketplace. If you have sufficient profit margins, you should consider Amazon. They take a healthy fee, but then again you can become part of Amazon's amazing shipping system, where they handle the delivery in a day or two to just about anyone, anywhere.

Etsy has exploded as a place for independent shops to display their goods. If you have customers who spend a lot of time on Facebook, then its Marketplace platform will allow you to sell physical products.

All of these services have the potential to deliver sales during slower periods, and you can instantly expand or contract your presence on them.

The Most Dangerous Number in Business

This is a good time to talk about the number that, in my opinion, has caused more business failures than any other. That most dangerous number is "one."

When you have one way to bring in business, you're skating on thin ice. Maybe you're selling a ton on Amazon, until Amazon changes its policies, or creates its own in-house product, or something else happens.

Maybe you have a business where you get a ton of customers from one place, like Facebook or the big lumber mill on the edge of town—until the mill closes or Facebook becomes way too expensive. Or, as I mentioned earlier, you could rely solely on word of mouth, which by itself is not a marketing plan.

As we saw in Season 4, Episode 2 at Whilma's Filipino Restaurant, Whilma Frogoso worked super-long hours as the only chef. She succeeded at it, but it was taking a big toll on her. It also meant that she could never take a break.

You might have one single supplier for an important component to your product or service. Not only could that supplier go away for whatever reason, but what kind of pricing are you getting? As we discussed earlier, in order to get competitive pricing, you want to make sure that suppliers know that you do a bit of shopping around.

When you're thinking about how you bring in business, does one of the methods you listed represent by far the primary way you get business? If so, it's important that you diversify. That does not necessarily mean cutting back on the primary way, but instead adding to it.

In this chapter, I outlined many concepts and things to try. As noted earlier in this book, no one knows the exact right assortment of marketing/social/promotion choices. But you can find out by trying many different options and combinations.

I encourage you to try and try again to find the right combinations. It will be worth it.

~~~

No matter what methods you use to bring in business, you need to be effective in persuading people that you deserve their business. That's what we discuss next.

7

The Craft of Persuasion

IF YOU ASK people who know me how they might describe me, you'll sometimes hear: "Barry's a sales guy." That certainly is one of the many hats I wear proudly. But here's the thing:

We all are salespeople. And as business owners, we *must* be persuasive salespeople. If you can't represent your business in a compelling way, who will?

"Hang on!," you protest. "I'm not a salesperson, I'm an artist. I have a pottery studio and I only display my works. I never push them on people." Pushing is different than selling. When pushing, someone is making another person uncomfortable enough to act in a way not in their own interest. In selling, you are sharing the benefits of a product and matching those benefits with the customer's needs in a persuasive way. Pushing and persuasively selling are different things.

I do understand the aversion to "pushing." But if you have decided you are above persuading others that your product or service is best, or you are unwilling to represent yourself or your product aggressively, you will likely never be a successful businessperson.

If you really believe in a product or service, and really believe it is the right solution for a customer, when you "sell" a product you are simply sharing your conviction that the product is right for a customer.

Without selling, there are no sales and there is no business. At its root, business is about selling. As outlined earlier, accept and make peace with this along with all the other realities of being a business owner.

You know this already in your heart. All day long you are in the persuasion business. It may start with getting your dog to sit while you put a leash on them. It continues with encouraging a family member to take a certain action, and this is before you even get to your studio.

You have a new employee who came from a different studio. You'll need to meet with her to explain how you do not sell your pottery the way that other studio did. Oh, and after lunch you need to meet with your web designer because your site is not properly showcasing your latest Snowdrift line of pottery glazes. And let's face it, even as an artist, if you want to make a living at your craft you are in business. You are creating something with the explicit idea that someone will like it and buy it. That is persuasion. That is professional selling.

You're in sales, all right. It's just that Madison Avenue and Hollywood have done their best to give sales a checkered reputation. You don't have to look beyond big movies like *The Wolf of Wall Street* or the famous "Always Be Closing" sales scene in *Glengarry Glen Ross*.

I called this chapter The Craft of Persuasion because it comes closer to describing the skill that's absolutely central to small and big businesses alike. At one end of the persuasion spectrum are the hucksters who bully, cajole, and trick people into buying. I want to talk about the other end of the spectrum, where customers are only too happy to be ambassadors for a business because of the amazing way they're treated each time they visit.

I believe I can hear you thinking: *Well, okay, "persuasion" is a better word in my mind than "sales." Even so, it has overtones of making people do what they don't want to do, and that's not me at all.*

I get that the last thing you're going to do is shove your product down the throat of a customer who does not want it. I feel the same way. What I'm talking about is so much more ethical and sophisticated. Here's how I define it:

In business, persuasion is thoroughly knowing your customer, and then honestly presenting your offerings in the best light. You make it easy for your target customer to see your value. Sales will follow.

Are you onboard with that? Good, because it can be used in so many situations, and it will transform your business into a powerhouse, both online and face-to-face.

11 Principles of Business Persuasion

The great thing about these principles is most of them work independently. That means even if you do half of them effectively, you'll be way ahead of the game. And if you do them all—well, your competition will be left scratching their heads at how you can capture so much of the market.

Principle #1: Speak to One Person

When you're shaking hands with someone, you make eye contact at the same time. But what if you're looking at that person and he's looking off somewhere else? How does that make you feel?

That's basically the same thing that easily 95 percent of people do in their text and videos. Once you get what I'm talking about, you'll see it *everywhere*, multiple times per day. The way it happens is the speaker addresses a group, and not an individual. Here are just some of the telltale signs in language:

- "Good morning, everyone!"
- "Some of you may be wondering whether. . . ."
- "I bet many of you feel that. . . ."
- "You are some of my best customers."

Yes, many thousands of copies of this book have been printed and I understand that in one sense I'm speaking to a group. But I've been careful to do my best to make this book be a conversation between two people—you and me. Not a blob of people and me. The way I look at it, whether you're reading this book, watching a video of me, or listening to a podcast, you are doing me the honor of paying attention to me. Why should I disrespect you by continuously signaling that you're some mass of people?

On a few occasions it makes perfect sense to address a group. In Season 3, Episode 8, Ty Pennington, the *SBR* co-host, said: "All of you guys working together to make a better town is making America a better place to be." That makes perfect sense. It truly *is* a crowd in front of him and he's making a point about group effort. I do the same thing in town hall meetings with our employees. I'll say: "Hey gang, it's Barry . . ." before getting into our conversation.

But that's a rare type of interaction. You should review all of your emails, videos, and automated texts and see where you are not speaking to one person. Instead of "Dear Dog Lovers," say "Dear Dog Lover." Instead of saying "Everyone who fills out this form will be entered into our Cookie Raffle," say "When you fill out this form, we'll enter you into our Cookie Raffle."

During the pandemic, I got into listening to podcasts on occasion. One of my favorites is called *Smartless* with actors Jason Bateman, Sean Hayes, and Will Arnett. One of their running jokes is that they refer to their audience as "listener," as if they have only one. Though it is a running skit, they are trying to make a point: although they have millions of followers, they can still speak to you as an individual, and it's effective.

Every day, thousands of customers across the United States and Canada call one of our call centers, either to reorder a printed product, ask a question about their website, or to purchase something from our promotional solutions division. When they call, they speak to an individual: one of our call-center representatives. The interaction is one-on-one, and so is the solution: "Yes, we can add payroll services for your employees, Ms. Anderson." It creates a justifiable expectation about how people prefer to be treated.

We live in an age in which almost all the communication we receive in a day is mass-produced and targeted to huge numbers of people, and it shows. That's partly why COVID was so tough—it took away a lot of one-to-one communication. Don't contribute to the mass-communication noise, and instead make your voice stand out by speaking to an individual.

Principle #2: Get to Know Your Customer More Than You Do Today

Notice how I did *not* say merely: "Know your customer," because lots of people will reflexively say, "Hey, I know my customer!"

Knowing your customer is a little like knowing the weather. It's constantly changing, and you can always learn more. That's why Harvey Mackay required his salespeople to come back with one additional bit of customer knowledge each time they went on a sales call, as we discuss elsewhere.

We do the same thing: we have salespeople across the country who call on customers each day. They know their business, their families, and often their entire stories. Small-business owners need to do the same.

Let's say you knew your customers pretty well before the big-box store moved into town. You still may know them the same amount, but their buying calculations may have just changed: *We're tight on cash this month and I can get the same product for less money at Big Box than I can downtown. Hmmm. . . .*

For another example, look at how Amazon has utterly changed expectations for delivery of products. If you're older than about 20, you'll vividly remember the bad old days: you order a product and might be told *after* you order: "Oops, sorry, it's on backorder." Even if it was in stock, you would wait several days to maybe get a notice that your product finally shipped. Then it was a guessing game about when it would show up.

Amazon changed the entire expectation framework of all those customers—the ones who businesses said they knew so well. Now something is slow if it arrives in three days. And if you want it in one day or even the same day in some situations, Amazon can arrange it.

The world has shifted underneath our feet, and so have customer expectations. That's why it's all about getting to know your customers continuously better, lest they drift away.

I have to make a point here: it's true that Amazon is amazing at how it has revolutionized quick shipping, but it was not the pioneer at quick shipping. Deluxe was. Years before Jeff Bezos entered kindergarten, Deluxe had an amazing supply chain, and you probably experienced it yourself.

In the bad old days, pretty much all products were shipped in the slow, plodding fashion I mentioned before—except for your bank checks. You might remember how you filled out the little form at the end of your last checkbook and gave it to the bank teller. Then in a fraction of the time it took for anything else to appear in your mailbox, you got the black-red-and-white Deluxe box of checks.

Even more amazing was that this was not a generic box of stuff where thousands of pallets could sit in warehouses around the country, ready for shipment. The checks were personalized and printed just for you. We basically invented the concept of "mass customization." I just think that's a cool example of an industry leader doing what it takes to provide an unusual level of service to customers.

So how do you get to know your customer in a continuously deeper way? First, you stop thinking *I know my customers* and you start thinking *How can I find out more about what my customers are thinking and doing?*

You have many ways to do that. When it comes to some of your best customers, a good way is to pick up the phone. Here's another story from master salesman Joe Girard.

A guy came to his dealership and was ready to buy a car that was fully loaded with every accessory. Things were going great, until the guy suddenly excused himself and left. Joe couldn't figure out what had gone wrong, so he decided to call the customer. The customer said that right before he was ready to sign the papers for the car, he made some comments about how proud he was for his son, and he noticed that Joe had no interest. Joe acted like he had already made the sale and was patiently waiting for this stuff about the customer's son to be over. And that was why the customer bought a car elsewhere.[1]

Even if there is no similar issue in your case with a sale or missed sale, you should be in regular contact with your best customers. Many of the businesses in *SBR* had no problem doing this. But you may be an online business, where it's a little difficult to step out of the kitchen and circulate around the dining room in your restaurant or bar.

In that case, you will flatter your best customers if you send them a personalized note that does not start off: "Dear Valued Customers." If you're an online business, send a personalized email that *proves* the note is personalized.

You can do that by referring to a recent detail. A friend of mine has bought replacement printer toner for years from a company. Recently he got a personalized note that said: "Hi, I first want to thank you for being a customer for the last 6 years, when your first order was on March 6, 2015. I also want to thank you for the 16 orders you've made since then! But I also noticed that you have not ordered from us in the last 9 months. Therefore, I wanted to write and see if it was something we did or didn't do that made you not order. . . ."

Wow, right? As a customer, this letter would make you feel important, and like your business mattered. Have you ever received a letter like that? I haven't. Yet it cost next to nothing for the company to do a little bit of programming of its customer database and issue those emails. The message to take away from this example is: "What could I do relatively quickly to stay in regular touch with my best customers, and ask them what's on their mind?"

Surveys Done the Right Way. Surveys are also far underused. We all have been subjected to poorly done surveys that say things like: "It's super important for us to get five-star ratings from our loyal customers like all of you. . . ." That may be kind of effective in collecting meaningless five-star "you rock" kind of ratings.

But if you're genuinely interested in getting suggestions for improvement from your customers, there's a better way. You need to give people permission to be honest with you. Say something like: "Thanks so much for attending our self-defense course yesterday. Please let us know the best part of the event, in your opinion." Then after whatever other questions you want to ask, say: "Of course nothing is perfect. Though we tried to make this as good an event as we could, we'd love your honest opinion about what we could have done better. Please be brutally honest; we love direct feedback."

Very few companies give permission like that for candid feedback, yet that's going to be some of the best guidance you'll ever receive for becoming more profitable over time. First, the customers will be impressed that you wanted candid feedback and respect you and your business more. People generally want to be helpful. If their feedback is heard, and acted upon, it also can create tremendous loyalty. Second, if the competitive landscape has changed and your customers have new expectations, this is a great way to find that out. And third, it will help prevent what we in the Midwest call "Minnesota nice." This is when you word a survey in such a way that people tell you what you want to know. People will just click 5 out of 5 to be nice, but that doesn't give you what you need to know. Wording the survey to gain actual feedback is critical.

Of course, some of the feedback you get from surveys will be bogus. It's just a fact of life that some people are unreasonable, or worse. You could put on the most amazing event and someone will rate you lower because it rained that day, or you didn't offer enough free champagne or whatever. That's not a reason to avoid doing surveys.

Principle #3: Know Your Competition and Find a Way to Outclass Them

I've talked a little about this before, and I'll make some different points here. First, just as your customers change, so does your competition. Therefore, you'll never be done with this process. It's ethical to visit their websites and even sign up for their newsletters, because it's not unethical for them to do that to you.

As much as it feels right to stick to your own knitting and not be looking at what competitors are doing, that's a mistake. Any customer who is being prudent will do research, determine who are the best suppliers of products and services, and then make a judgment about which ones get the business. That's why *Consumer Reports* magazine exists, and why Amazon has made so many billions off its system of reviews. People want help with product comparisons.

Yet think about when you've been a customer and you've asked a business something like, "Could you please tell me how your roofing service compares to other companies?" You'll often hear: "Oh, we have a policy of not criticizing our competitors." What a cop-out! That's usually when I turn around and leave. I didn't ask them to dump on the competition, but instead to give me factual differences. When I hear the "no-criticism policy" stuff, I suspect one of two things: either they don't stack up so well versus the competition, or they're too lazy to keep track of them. Or both.

It's so much more believable to say, "I'm glad you asked. Your house is in Colorado and you know how we get hailstorms here like nobody's business. We put a special liner under the shingles that gives them the ability to absorb some shock from above. It's true that it costs a little bit more, but we've found that it results in way fewer callbacks after hailstorms. We're the only company in Colorado that uses the roof liner as standard equipment."

Now that's useful! Maybe I don't care about hailstorms because my insurance company will pay for damage. But at least I'm given a specific, factual difference. I also have a little comfort that they're keeping tabs on the competition, which makes me feel like I don't have to do some of that comparison homework.

Importantly, if you don't have a verifiable advantage that you can defend, you need to work on one quickly. "Me-too" products invite intense price competition, leading to many business failures.

But differentiation isn't always just about product. It can be about attitude, service, and desire to win—essentially outclassing the competition in the competition itself.

A good friend of mine started and ran a successful software and digital signage business for movie cinemas. He ultimately sold this business for a very attractive price.

He tells a story about how his young company began by winning big cinema contracts, beating much larger competitors. Instead of showing up with just PowerPoint slides describing their solution, they shipped the actual terminals and/or monitors used in the cinema to the presentation site. The team used the actual devices to demonstrate the software's flexibility and ease of use in its actual installed environment. The competition showed up just with PowerPoint slides, talking about their market leadership and company stability. Who would you buy from?

My friend's company won again and again. Yes, they had a better product, but the competition had a stronger balance sheet and a reference list a mile long. The young company demonstrated how much they wanted the business, how they were scrappy, and they convinced the customer they were the right partner.

This is outclassing the competition.

Principle #4: Write Like You Talk, and Talk Like a Friend

Perhaps you've noticed the informal conversational style of this book. I have always been more successful presenting a topic in language everyone understands. It's more authentic, more approachable, and more engaging.

Sometimes, things can get mucked-up. For example, I love my legal team at Deluxe, and they're indispensable. But I could never be an attorney, because I want to tell people what I know, when I know it, in plain English.

Here's an example—not from Deluxe, but it's the way someone else wrote:

> I am herewith returning the stipulation to dismiss in the above entitled matter; the same being duly executed by me.[2]

You can't persuade people if they've already died from boredom, or if they simply have no idea of what you just said. Of course, we don't have space here to discuss good writing in any depth. What I suggest is that you do a little soul searching here. Yes, we all learned how to write. That does not make us good at it. Do you really get into writing and regularly are looking for ways to get better at it? In that case, maybe you're all set.

But if you're like most people, writing feels like a medium-to-large chore. You can get better at it by using some of the sophisticated tools out there now like Grammarly.com and ProWritingAid.com. They can catch a ton of mistakes and will also make suggestions that increase readability and style. They're not perfect, but they go a long way toward giving you specific suggestions for improving what you write.

Another way to write like you talk is to get most of it down by talking. People who use Pixel phones have access to the Google Recorder app, which is remarkable. It's like some *Star Trek* scene where you can turn it on, ask it to transcribe, and watch as the words you say are poured as text onto the screen in real time. It's also remarkably accurate. There probably is the equivalent for whatever other type of phone you have.

But even if you have to record your speaking and get it transcribed, it may be worth it. If you like to speak much more than you care to write, then start talking. This is a great way to get a lot of material on paper relating to the product features you like most, the great event coming up that customers shouldn't miss, your tips for getting dogs ready to travel, and so on.

Once you have the bulk of it down, it's a snap to edit. You could even take that spoken transcript and run it through the style checkers I mentioned earlier; that would leave very little cleanup.

Let's face it, most small-business owners can't afford a professional copywriter to help write emails or web pages, or to respond to reviews. It is your business, and it has to be your voice. We have worked with millions of small businesses over the years, and the most successful are the ones that have the personality of the owner in the messages they deliver.

Principle #5: Own a Phrase in Your Customers' Heads

There's a really good book called *The Micro-Script Rules*, by Bill Schley.[3] In it he says that it's not what you tell people that counts, and it's not what they hear. It's what they repeat to other people. I've heard this concept similarly described as "not what you say in a speech they will remember, instead it will be how the speech made you feel."

It's pretty clear that Ohm Nohm Bakery & Cafe in Season 5, Episode 5 owned the customer mind space for "gluten-free baked goods." It's also clear that Lovett's in Season 3, Episode 5 owned the terms "snoots" and "soul food" in the minds of people near Alton, Illinois.

My team was honest when it came to Lovett's and heard the term "snoots." It was not something they were familiar with, and they didn't know what to make of it at first. As the marketing team came together to discuss how to position Lovett's, they at first wanted to do away with the idea of sharing snoots with the general public. That would have been a mistake. In the Alton area, and indeed in the South, it is a well-known term and Lovett's owned it. It is definitely part of their story and an incredibly important term for them to own.

What can *you* own? This partly gets to the branding discussion we had in Chapter 4. It's another case of a moving target for most businesses, as the marketplace changes. Amazon started out wanting to be known as the "Earth's Biggest Bookstore" and they've morphed into what people most likely would say is the earth's biggest store, period.

Deluxe is the original payments company, having invented the check-book, but for the longest time, we were only known as the checkbook people. These days we are a trusted payments and business technology company, one that champions business so communities thrive. We are also a partner to companies large and small.

You can be known for different things, too. For example, Schlem-mer Brothers in Season 1, Episode 5 is owned by Kent Henderson. They've been around for more than a century, and they firmly own hearths, grills, stoves, and fireplaces in the mind of anyone within driv-ing distance. Kris White managed that business, but Kent also works to be seen as the go-to business for any kind of metalworking in the area.

Having a crisp idea of what you want to be known for means that you can reinforce it at every turn—in your branding, in what you talk about in social media, the sales events you have, and so on.

Principle #6: Talk about the Benefits of Benefits

I can hear you going: *Huh?* Stick with me because this is an advanced concept that you can use immediately.

If you look around at most advertising, it's pitiful. It consists mostly of headlines that the business cares about, not the customer. For exam-ple, "Clearance Event" is what the business wants to do to move all its unsold inventory, or "Free Retirement Seminar" is when you're going to be pitched some investment. Big whoop.

One notch up from that is the headline that talks about features: "Our new X-12 LED bulb draws only 14 watts" or "The Acme saw blade has 50 teeth" or "Our system will deliver to you unlimited amounts of deionized water to wash your vehicle." Uh huh.

You will separate yourself from most of your competitors if you talk about benefits and not features. The way to look at this is that people do not go to the hardware store to buy quarter-inch drill bits. They go there because they want quarter-inch holes. The drill bit is the feature, and the hole is the benefit.

Therefore, I could say "The X-12 bulb draws only 14 watts, so that has the potential to cut your lighting bill by 70 percent." I could also explain how having more teeth on a saw blade results in a smoother cut, and deionized water means the car will dry without any water spots. Those are all things that customers may actually care about.

So, what did I mean when I said "talk about the benefits of benefits"? This is rarely done but highly effective. You bring home the benefit by talking about how it will feel to the customer:

> ". . . and with that 70 percent savings on your lighting bill, you'll not only save money but can rest easy that you're doing your part for the environment."

> ". . . smoother cuts mean less time sanding, and more time building the furniture you've always wanted."

> "Your vehicle will not only avoid water spots, but people at the car convention will crowd around, asking about your secrets to that impressive finish."

Whether it's wrenches or college educations, people don't buy things for the sake of things; they buy them for what those things will do for them. Whenever you can, try to connect the dots between what you offer and the emotions they can generate in your customers.

When you communicate the benefits in advertising, be sure the benefit and your brand are what the potential customer remembers. Do a little test to prove the point to yourself. Next time you're driving down the road, look at all the billboards. After you can no longer see a particular billboard, ask yourself, What did the billboard advertise? Why do you care about what they were advertising? You will find the significant majority of the time you won't recall what you saw or the benefit being offered.

Sometimes the billboard will have the picture of a professional-looking real estate agent covering 80 percent of the billboard, but you can't see the agent's name. What is the benefit the agent is offering—they have a professional appearance? How does that sell houses? Why would you choose that person to sell your house, when you don't a reason to choose them and you can't even see their name?

Instead, imagine that same billboard with a message: Susan Jones Realty. Fast sale. Fair price. Fantastic service. Phone number, Website.

Principle #7: Prove Every Assertion

As they say, if I only had a nickel for every time this was violated. . . .

It's fine if you make claims for your product or service. It's even fine if you make outlandish claims. What is not fine is making them and then moving on. *You must prove them.*

You can't be online for more than five minutes and not see ads that make all sorts of great claims. Just think about it: if you believed in your bones that the diet plan worked as they described, you'd whip out your credit card in a flash. And how about that dating seminar that promises to attract that special someone to you like a "super magnet on steroids"? Sold! So, what's stopping you from becoming broke in an afternoon?

Your intuition stops you. By now you have seen more than 500,000 or so ads and you have a finely tuned ability to ignore anything that's not fully supported. Of course, the lower the cost, the looser the filter. If you sell blueberry muffins, you might not have to say too much beyond "We only use wild Maine blueberries."

If you make expensive leather luggage, the bar is higher. If you want me to pay $800 for a suitcase, you have two choices: (1) Get a photo of Taylor Swift with your luggage, and it'll be sold out in one afternoon; or (2) Explain to me why your bag is so superior to others on the market.

No one does that better with luggage than SaddlebackLeather. com. Their superb tagline is "They'll fight over it when you're dead." Go to YouTube and type in: "Saddleback leather tannery" and you'll see some pretty explicit but great videos about how cowhide turns into leather. You'll also hear about all the shortcuts other leather companies make to sell cheaper stuff.

You may or may not be interested in leather products. Either way, study this guy for how he makes informative videos that explain how the cheap guys do things, and how the quality people do them. You can adapt this approach to your business, whether you're a florist, bakery, printer, or real estate agent.

To summarize, explainer videos are incredibly good for proof. You can use other forms, too. As I mentioned before, testimonials are an excellent form of social proof. Another good method is to use statistics. For example, if you say your restaurant only serves USDA Prime beef, then explain how only 2 to 5 percent of beef in the United States is classified at the top level of Prime.

If you have dozens of whiskeys available at your pub, then make an effort to see if anyone else in the state has more. This should be an easy online search. Then you can say: "To our knowledge, we have the largest selection of Irish whiskeys in the state." That statement is not only a form of proof, but it also qualifies as a phrase you can own in the mind of customers.

Principle #8: Explain Who Is Not Right for Your Product or Service

As I said before, absolutely nothing is the best fit for everyone. We all know that. Why then do businesses claim that their widget is "revolutionary" and is "the only one you'll ever need"? Because that's what they want you to think. That transfers the burden to the customer of figuring out when the widget is the best choice and when it is not, because it simply can't be best for everyone. The businesses think the louder they shout about their offerings, the more people will buy them. That persuades no one.

Let's say you offer lawn-care services. I will not believe you if you say, "We offer the best, lowest-cost lawn care for any size lawn in the tri-state area." I'm thinking: *Oh really? So you could take care of the lawn at Wrigley Field in Chicago and you'll also do my lawn at the lowest cost? I don't think so.*

I would be much more inclined to believe you if you said, "If your lawn is between 100 square feet and one acre, we're the choice for you. We can apply our special five-step process to your lawn so you can focus on getting your hammock ready to go. Your neighbors will not know your secret to leisurely lawn care."

Principle #9: Reverse the Risk

In any business transaction, one party takes more risk than the other. Some businesses make it clear with their "NO REFUNDS" sign that you, the consumer, are taking all the risk. A few others will have "iron-clad" guarantees where you can return the product for whatever reason for a full refund within a certain period.

It doesn't take a detective to read wildly positive language about how something is revolutionary and the "only one you'll ever need," yet notice the lousy guarantee. It probably is for only 15 days, and requires you to call ahead for a "Return Merchandise Authorization" plus to ship it back with all tags in completely unused condition, and they'll maybe think of refunding you—slowly—after they keep a 15 percent "restocking fee."

I don't know about you, but after I'm forced to jump through all those hoops to return a lousy product, I make a mental note to never work with that company again. I also will tell anyone who'll listen how bad the company is. But I'm also fair about it: if someone treats me well and accepts a return for a full refund within a generous period, they pretty much have my business forever.

It's a balancing act. It's true that a few customers will take advantage of you. This gets back to our one-sheet accounting process in Chapter 2. If you know your numbers, you can run a test where you offer a great return policy. Then you can measure how many people take advantage of you, offset by how many people are delighted customers who spend more with you. This is a process that your competitors are highly unlikely to be even aware of, never mind implement. As a result, you can grow your business and they'll be left wondering what happened.

Principle #10: Remove Speed Bumps to the Sale

The best companies on the planet make it really smooth and easy for you to work with them. They have teams of people who focus on the customer experience in great detail, and they look for ways to improve it. In the *SBR* series, you'll sometimes see these people as part of the team at Deluxe. They're known by the acronyms CX for customer experience, and UX for user experience.

Maybe you don't have a team at your disposal, but that's okay. The key concept here is to look at your products and services from the perspective of your target customers, and to identify issues or speed bumps.

For example, tell me that these situations have never happened to you:

- You received a product like a bowl, pot, or tool, and it had a price sticker that would not come off cleanly. It tore apart and you spent 15 minutes cleaning off the adhesive, while getting angrier the whole time. Some first impression.

- You filled out a form online and were about to hit "submit" after going off to gather some of the details. The form timed out, it wiped out the information you entered, and then told you that you must start over—you took too long.
- You filled out a form that asked you for a password with no guidance. You supplied one, and only then were you told: "Bad password. You must use at least one lowercase letter, one uppercase letter, one symbol, and it must be at least eight characters long. . . ."

I'm just scratching the surface, right? It's infuriating how some companies seemingly don't spend any time looking at their products and experiences from the customers' perspective. If you do spend the time, your customers will love you for it; plus they'll tell their friends what a smooth experience they've had with you.

You can improve that experience with your products and services in two ways:

Method 1. Walk through the process yourself. This can be online or at a physical location. The Japanese have taken this process to an art form. They call it Gemba, which is translated as "the real place." To take a Gemba walk is to try to look at an operation from a perspective you have not taken before.[4]

For example, try to buy a product online. See where something is confusing, maybe in the shopping cart. If you notice that anything at all is slowing you down, or requiring extra clicks, you can be sure that a customer will have an even harder time.

Method 2. Watch as others walk through your physical location or online presence. This is called "user testing" in the business and it's super valuable. You may have gone through your site or looked at your store, and everything makes sense to you. That's not surprising, given how it's your business. But to see it through the eyes of a newcomer is sometimes humbling and informative.

In the case of your online site, you can ask a friend to let you watch as she's given a task to do on your site. For example, you can say, "Please try to buy a floral arrangement for a wedding." Then you shut up, give no help or commentary at all, and take notes. It's also very useful if you ask your friend to think aloud. She may say:

"Okay, I chose the arrangement. Where do I put it in the cart? I don't see a button anywhere. Oh . . . I have to scroll down to see the button!" Then later, in the shopping cart, she says, "It says I have three things in the cart. I only wanted one. What are the other two? How can I get rid of them?"

You may get frustrated yourself, because you're standing there, and you must not say anything, but you want to say to her: "Come on! The button's right there, plain as day! Why can't you see it?"

This is why user testing is so amazingly valuable. You get to see your business in a new light, and now you can fix some of those things. They have the potential to increase sales without any additional advertising.

Another entirely different type of speed bump to sales is lack of training on the part of staff. If you're tracking key numbers like revenues, then you may see a pattern, where sales seem to be lower on the days when a certain person is on duty, compared with other days. You might even get more customer comments about one person versus another.

It's easy to dismiss such comments as coming from too-sensitive customers. After all, your cousin Augie is a little rough around the edges, but he does know his stuff. The problem is that a lack of complaints is not a good gauge for anything. Think about your own experience: Do you sometimes leave a place and resolve never to come back, yet you don't lodge a complaint? Sometimes it's just not worth the bother.

In that context, if someone does comment about Augie, it could be that for every 20 people who are annoyed, only one bothers to comment. This all gets back to the Russian proverb to "trust but verify." Trust your staff but develop a high level of attention to any clues that maybe things are not running as well as you hope and need them to.

Some businesses discover shocking things when they see their business through the eyes of mystery shoppers (you can google the term). These are people who will walk into your store, or call your business to make an appointment. They go through all the motions and then report back to the business owner what they found. It may seem like spying on your staff, but in my opinion there's nothing unethical about it. In fact, it's an opportunity for great people to be recognized.

I heard of a case where a dental practice offered dental implants. These are high-tech alternatives to dentures, where replacement teeth can be made and individually installed in the jaw as a permanent solution. They look just like real teeth. Anyway, they're expensive. The owner of the dental practice hired a mystery shopper to see what the experience was like to book an appointment. To his horror, the mystery shopper reported back that she went through the process of booking an appointment and the staff person lowered her voice and said: "Look, you really don't want to get these implants, okay? They're so expensive!"

This type of experience is important not only in a small business, but also in extremely large ones. When I started as CEO at Deluxe, I asked some high-potential members of our team to act as customers and call some of our people, from sales to administration to some of my leaders. I wanted to see what the experience was like. Did we live our values? Did we always return calls or emails in a timely manner? Were we professional? To their credit, the majority of people who work for us provided exceptional customer service, but a few fell down, badly. We worked on it, because you can *always* improve your customer service.

Principle #11: Don't Be Boring

Sometimes businesses have complex products or services that need a lot of explanation. They will wring their hands about what they should do, because they fear that the web page or written page will be too long. I have news for them: there's no such thing as too long a description— only a description that is too boring.

Here in Minnesota, we boast about being the land of 10,000 lakes, which means that people love their outdoor activities. For discussion, let's say I'm one of them and I have been saving up for a couple of years for an all-terrain vehicle. I've talked with my buddies and have narrowed the search down to the Arctic Cat, Polaris, and Yamaha brands. I finally have enough dough scraped up for a top-of-the-line baby, and the time has come. The only question is a particular model from Arctic Cat or Polaris versus that new ATV that Yamaha just announced.

Do you think for a moment that I am going to be bored reading page after page of details about each ATV? Plus maybe 50 or so reviews? Absolutely not. In fact, as I read, I see myself doing the things the reviewers talk about. It's part of the fun.

Now if I sit down with what I think will be cool product descriptions and they're written in a boring way, then I may not be so inclined to purchase. Sure, the actual warranty and other legal disclaimers need to be written in a language that will never be mistaken for being animated. But the sales text should never be boring.

Whatever products or services you sell, do an informal audit of whether their descriptions are boring or lively. Are there stories? Is the text broken up with images? Are you being talked to directly, or is it the "some of you may be thinking" jazz that I mentioned in Principle #1?

Do you have a Frequently Asked Questions (FAQ) section? If so, are they softball questions, or do they have an edge to them, as if written by a skeptical consumer?

Key point: I have no patience with cynics, but I love skeptics. A cynic is someone who's long on opinion and sour attitudes, but often short on real insight or experience. It's the continuous "glass is half empty" mentality that wears on me. But skeptics are open-minded people who don't yet know if something is right for them. They need proof. I'm a skeptic.

So, when you write a FAQ, load it up with questions the skeptic might ask. For example, in Season 5, Episode 7, we met Julie LaGrow, Executive Director of Literacy Volunteers of Chautauqua County (LVCC). A lot of her job is running the literacy center, but she also must be involved in fundraising. Now that's a hard job.

If I'm writing an FAQ from a skeptic's perspective, I might write these sorts of questions:

- Some charities spend an awful lot of money on overhead and other things that are not directly helping the people in need. How does LVCC stack up in this regard?
- Is the literacy work you do something that's nice but not much more than that, or is it really making a material difference in people's lives? How can you tell?
- Aren't there other programs that the local schools have and some others that are administered by the state? Is LVCC actually filling a need?

You get the idea. The questions have a bit of an edge to them and they come across as real straight talk. Those tend to make people nod to themselves and become engaged.

~~~

At different points in this book I have talked about how certain tasks are never finished. Practicing these persuasion principles is another example. In fact, few activities of a business owner will have a higher payoff than being able to attract your target customers and persuade them through the online and physical messages you create.

Once you do get the attention of potential new customers and persuade them to check you out, you need a whole set of skills to develop that curiosity into something stronger. That's what we discuss next.

8

Relationships

Relax. I'm Not going to get into those *other kinds* of relationships here. Instead, I want to talk about your relationships with leads, prospects, and customers.

We just have gone through quite a long list of places where you can be visible, and you should have made a list of everywhere you currently are visible and some of the places that may be worth adding to your mix.

Next, I want to make some important distinctions between the different statuses or profiles of people who take an interest in your business. This is crucial because in my experience, many businesses think of people in a binary way: my current buyers, and everyone else.

This is illustrated by a friend of mine who was in the market for a new car a few years ago. He had a young family with three kids and showed up at a dealership one day. The couple had done their homework and knew not only the brand of vehicle they wanted, but the exact model and even the trim package. Oh, and they were paying cash, which in those days was considered good.[1] The only decision was the color of the van.

The salesman had been in the business for years, and treated them well through the buying process. They shook hands and left. My friend says that 20 years later, he has yet to hear from the salesman since the day they bought that van.

Just think about that for a minute. The buyers knew exactly what they wanted, so the selling process was quick and really only an order-taking process. They paid cash. The salesman might wonder: *Hmmm, would this be the only car they need? Maybe both of them commute to work?* The salesman didn't bother to do any fact finding.

This "experienced" salesman left no pile of business cards in the glove compartment, the way we heard Joe Girard did. He didn't call up a week later to see how the van was working, and to thank them again for the purchase. He didn't spend five minutes to send a brief thank-you note, with business cards. After all, owners of new cars may take pride in the purchase and talk with friends, some of whom may be in the market for one.

It did not occur to this guy that many people go through vehicles rather quickly, either because they wreck them, they decide they don't like the car after all, or they just always like to drive new models. No "Happy Holidays" card from this guy.

It also never dawned on this "professional" that kids grow up and want cars of their own. Some parents even buy them cars. Let's give this guy the benefit of the doubt and conclude that shortly after the sale, he was run over by a bus. Even then, his manager would know about this recent purchase and could have assigned someone to follow up on this new customer, with potentially many additional sales over 20 years.

Nope. This dealership pays attention to current buyers who walk in the showroom, and no one else. The thing is, on the face of it, the transaction was fine. What was not fine was missing out on potentially 10 times the money of that original van purchase in later sales.

So you have Joe Girard, the greatest car salesman ever, who's rich and still takes the time to make each customer feel like a million bucks; and you have the local Joe Schmoe who no doubt goes home and grouses about how the dealership does not do enough marketing to bring in buyers.

You're probably not in the car game, so you might shrug at all of this. If you do, then you are entirely missing the point. In order to build that business of yours, let's spend some time thinking about the whole relationship timeline.

The Contact

A new relationship starts with a brief contact. Sometimes the contact is coincidental, like when you sit next to someone on the plane or at your kid's hockey game. "Hi, what do you do?" That's your first opportunity to make an impression.

There is a fable about a man walking by a construction site. He sees some bricklayers at work. He's kind of curious, so he asks the first bricklayer, "What are you doing?" The person said, "What does it look like? I'm laying brick."

He walked on a ways and asked the next bricklayer the same question. That person said, "I'm building a wall." He walked on down the road and found a third bricklayer. When he asked the same question, that person said, "I'm building a cathedral."

"So what do you do for a living?," I ask you when we're sitting in the bleachers, watching our kids. You could say, "I own a business downtown," or you could say, "I own that bakery down the street." Then again, you could say, "I own Ohm Nohm Bakery, and it's kinda unusual. We're the only truly gluten-free bakery in a nine-county area." Now that's a cathedral.

Think about your elevator speech; in other words, what you can say to someone about what you do, in the time it takes to ride a few elevator floors. What do you do? Okay, you might name the business, but *what do you really do **for** people?* What is the benefit they get from your business? We talked about this earlier, when we touched on your brand. You can never be "done" with this thought process, because marketplaces change, and so do customers and businesses.

Your elevator speech is your first chance to persuade a potential customer to consider your business. This is a form of selling, as outlined in the previous chapter.

One hundred years ago, if someone asked an employee of Deluxe "What do you do?," it would have been totally accurate for the person to say, "I work at Deluxe. We invented the checkbook, as well as new and more modern printing processes. Our engineers created incredible new business forms. And we pioneered the fast delivery of accurate checks to your door."

Today we still ship approximately 150,000 packages of checks *per day*, but that's only one of many services we offer. If I had to think of the very shortest, accurate answer to "So, what do you do?," I would say: "We are a technology company that helps businesses pay, get paid, optimize, and grow." The whole goal of a good elevator speech is to have someone say, "Oh? Tell me more."

The Thread

This initial contact could be at the sporting event I just described, but it could also be from your business card, the little ad you ran on Google, or from one of the other mechanisms we just went through.

If you've succeeded in generating a bit of curiosity on the part of the person concerning what you do, you've now created the thinnest of threads connecting that person with your business. That thread can now either be broken or strengthened.

Here's how you break the thread:

- You don't follow up with more information that creates further interest.
- You don't ask people any questions, so you're not in a position to know how to match your offerings with their situations.
- You blow it by making claims that you cannot back up. For example, if you say "we have the largest selection of lures and bait in the state" but your listener knows that not to be true.

If someone has just expressed a little bit of interest, I do not suggest that you pounce on them and close 'em hard. What I am suggesting is that you take some steps to add a thread to that thread, so it becomes a string, the start of an ongoing conversation.

Name Capture

Every so often you sit next to someone, strike up a conversation, and that person expresses at least a little interest in your business. Of course the logical thing to do in that situation is to hold out your hand and say, "Hi, I'm Barry." Then you find out the person's name and maybe you give her your card and use another card to write her name for your notes.

In contrast, in the online world you can have this happen every single day, and even dozens of times per day. We're talking about an effective name-capture mechanism. Here's how most businesses do it:

Almost all small businesses have nothing on their site to capture names. Oh, there might be an email address buried somewhere, so if I need to contact the business I can find a way. Instead, what I'm talking about is that most businesses do not have a specific, dedicated mechanism to attract and capture visitors' names.

"So what," you say? Visitors to your site or your business are precious. They represent future money and the future of your business. If they come to your site, look around, and leave without your having their contact information, then all you can do is hope that they'll be back.

Now think about your own Internet habits. If you're like me, you visit lots of sites daily. Maybe you're in the market for a new water heater. Your current one still works, but it makes these funny noises now and then. You search around and find an interesting site. You make a mental note or maybe add an online bookmark, and leave.

Months pass. Your water heater is kind of okay until you wake up one morning, turn on the shower to your normal setting, and step in. Whoa—you're awake in a hurry, because the water is barely warm. Ugh. That heater is definitely not long for this world.

You think about the research you've done on water heaters, and recall one particularly interesting site. You do another search, but you're on a different computer with a different browser, so you cannot look up your browsing history. Hey, time is now short, so you never do find that original site. Now you see something else that looks okay and you ask your plumber to order one, pronto.

Of the small percentage of sites that do have a name-capture mechanism, most of them do it in an ineffective manner. You see this on some sites: "Sign up for our FREE newsletter!"

That's what they want their visitors to do, and not what the visitors want. They're thinking: *Why should I sign up for just another newsletter? I get enough spam already. And big whoop—it's "free"— that's no reason to sign up. Besides, I'll remember the site if I need to return.* Ask yourself, how many times have you abandoned a site when you had to provide your contact information just to get basic information?

These days, having a "free newsletter" is about as remarkable as making a "toll-free call." The bar's been raised. People hate spam and you need to give them something of value in order to get their contact information. Here are some things you could do:

- Give them links to several previous newsletters, so they can see for themselves that they're useful.
- Even better: list several great topics that have been in recent newsletters, so they don't have to hunt through past issues.
- Offer to send them a handy checklist in exchange for their contact information. Maybe it could be: "Signs that your water heater may need replacing soon—and three signs that mean it could fail any day now."
- If you're a hair salon, it could be a handy list of ingredients that you should *never* allow in your shampoo if you want to keep your hair healthy.
- If you're an auto-detailing shop, you could send a list of low-cost products that will keep their vehicle's finish looking great between detailings.
- If you sell sporting goods, you could tell people that if they leave their name, you'll notify them for a special preview sale one week before next season's hottest gear is made available to the public.
- It could even be something like getting a discount or a free beverage.

It's very much worth your time to give people legitimate reasons for leaving their contact information. If you can think of none, then this is a great time to create some reasons.

In Season 1 Episode 7, we met Maria Smith, owner of the Eclectic Shop in Wabash, Indiana. Her business was to curate art and gifts from local artists and sell them to customers. Maria lacked a way to contact customers when new inventory came in. Because she was always curating new items in her shop, her customers could be fed a constant stream of potential new purchases, yet she didn't have a way to get in touch with them. We helped her build that connection point on her website, but also helped her keep a running list right at checkout. She didn't have to offer a newsletter, but simply could tell her customers that: "Hey, that artist whose item you just purchased is coming out with new designs in a week. If you write down your email address, I can let you know when they are in." Instantly, Maria had a new way *and* a reason to contact those customers.

Turning a Lead into a Prospect

If you've done a name capture, then the relationship is getting a little stronger. It's gone from simple curiosity to a small transaction—something of value in exchange for a name.

I go into more detail in Chapter 9 about what to do once you have the email addresses, because this concept can be such a game-changer for your business. For now, just note down whether you do any of the types of name capture mentioned earlier.

If you have a brick-and-mortar business, you can also make the connection to your customers stronger in a variety of ways.

One obvious way is to recognize when customers return to shop again. A friend of mine was in Reykjavik, Iceland, and stopped at a hole-in-the wall that served locally famous Belgian fries. They cook the fries to order so they take everyone's name and call them out when the order is ready. Well, my friend got some fries and they were so good that he decided to stop in the next day for more. The moment he walked in the door, the person working there said, "Hi Tom!" He was blown completely away. Here they must serve 200 people a day, and my friend had not even tipped him. Yet the person remembered his name. Talk about a focus on the customer.

That's the ultimate in building a feeling of rapport instantly, but it doesn't take a memory like that to impress people. Even if you have zero memory for names, you might remember faces and could say, "Hey, it's good to see you back!"

This is the time to begin to establish more of a two-way street, where both parties get to know each other better. You might ask if the person is looking for anything in particular, because you can order lots more than you have shelf space for. No matter how you engage the person, what you're doing is turning a lead into a prospect. That's the process of taking someone you know nothing about and finding out about them, so you can more appropriately help them.

Maybe someone stops by your dog-grooming center. If you engage the person you may discover that she's interested mainly in your dog-taxi service, and not in grooming. In that case, it would have been a waste to talk up grooming and give her a discount certificate for it. That can come later. For now, focus on what the customer wants, and get her name. You can then send her a series of emails over time with taxi-related topics like the best carriers, a discount code for the month of May, and so on.

Bobby Angelaccio does a great job of focusing on customers. Bobby owned Annabella's Restaurant in Bristol Borough, Pennsylvania. He was featured on Season 2 and was amazing at knowing what his customers wanted. One time our *SBR* crew was in for another great meal and the special was lobster risotto. Bobby knew one of our crew also loved a mix of seafood, so he quickly whipped up a seafood risotto with lobster, calamari, cuttlefish, and more. He remembered what our crew-member liked after only one visit and went out of his way to thrill her.

Leaning into this concept of building the relationship by learning more about your visitors has the potential to explode your business over time. How do I know? Think about your own experience as a customer. How many—or few—businesses take the time to know something about you, and become a helpful friend? Yeah, same here.

Relationships work in business when both people have a common interest and seek common benefits. Just because you want to sell Product X today doesn't mean this person is interested today or ever. Slow down, ask leading questions, and get to know the problem this person is trying to solve. If you can solve that person's problem, you've now found a potential new customer.

Remember, you're playing the long game. The goal is not to be the pushy, intrusive salesman who wants to close the deal with you today so he can make his monthly numbers. The goal is to be the helpful expert on whatever you do, so *of course* they'll buy from you when the time is right.

When Prospects Become Customers

If you take care of building relationships with the people who come in your physical or virtual door, they'll take care of building your business. It's true that some of them may never buy; perhaps a few people will come to your store to see things in person (or read all the good information you provide online) and then they buy from some discount house. There will always be a few of those. Then again, for every person like that, you'll get way more customers through word of mouth from the happy customer/ambassadors you've built a relationship with.

Of course, the relationship should just get stronger from here. Deluxe is headquartered in Minnesota, and there's another business in Minnesota that knows a thing or two about relationships—the MackayMitchell Envelope Company. Harvey Mackay worked lots of jobs when he was growing up, like selling magazines door to door, being a golf caddy, and selling envelopes. Long story short, Harvey became a sales legend, with seven books to hit the *New York Times* best-seller list.[2]

Harvey was world-class when it came to building relationships with customers. He created what he called the Mackay 66, which was a database of 66 things he wanted to learn about his customers. Imagine that: most businesses hardly bother to learn more than what they need in order to process a credit card. In contrast, the Mackay 66 had the names of spouse and kids, all the sports the family members played, the type of car the customer drove, vacation habits, hobbies—you get the idea.

Harvey had a rule: no salesperson could go out on a sales call to a customer and not return without adding one piece of information to the 66 list.

What did he do with all of this information? If Harvey met someone who played for a sports team—let's say the Dallas Cowboys—he would then look up in his database who loved Texas and the Cowboys, and he'd think of ways to connect them. If Harvey knew that someone served in the 101st Airborne Division and Harvey was going to meet a famous general from that division, he could arrange for the general to autograph a photo and send it to the customer.

Here this guy sold a simple commodity—envelopes. But he built an empire through steadily, appropriately growing his knowledge of his customers, who were only too happy to buy envelopes from him.

Maybe you don't know 66 things about your brother-in-law and think that's going overboard. Fine. Learn 33 things or even a dozen things about your customers, and you'll be the only one among your competitors to do so. This costs nothing but your interest and attention.

Lifetime Value of Customers

Do you know what your customers are worth? In one sense, of course you cannot put a price on people. Then again, some numbers can serve as good comparative measures.

For example, do you know how much your best customer has spent with you? If you had invoices in a shoebox and someone threw it out, then start keeping track now. Even if you have incomplete data, you should write down your top 10 percent or so of customers. As we talked about in Chapter 4, the whole world operates under some form of the 80/20 Principle. You name it, and most things are due to only a few things. Of the 15 dog chew toys you gave your dog, she probably likes a couple of them the most. You wear one or two garments more than you wear 30 others in your closet, combined.

You also have a handful of customers who represent a dispro-portionate share of your business to date. Who are they? Put them on paper, in order if you can. Does everyone in your company know how important these people are? Maybe you shouldn't distribute the rank order but you certainly could tell employees—and the customers themselves—that they're in the Inner Circle, or the Gold Club, or some other name you cook up for your best customers. Or you could just refer to them as "one of my best customers."

In addition to knowing about your best customers, you should know the lifetime customer value (LCV) for your business. That is the aver-age total amount that customers will spend for your type of product over their lifetimes. Check this out: by one measure, the LCV of a pizza parlor is *25,000 dollars*. And the average value of a customer to the Tropicana orange-juice folks is around $32,500.[3] Does that not blow you away?

That should shine a whole different light on customer interactions. First, let me get something off my chest: *the customer is not always right.* We're dealing with human beings and nobody is always right, period. Nevertheless, you get to decide if you want to keep the customer, and if you are willing to satisfy their need or demand. If you keep LCV in mind, rather than the value of a single pizza, you might respond dif-ferently to a complaint or demand. So many business owners get so caught up in the moment, focusing only on the immediate situation, they lose the insight of the lifetime value of a customer.

It's not a bad policy to delegate "yes" decisions to others, and reserve "no" decisions for your judgment. Here's how that works. You train your staff in the sorts of cases where they can go ahead and take care of the customer request themselves, if that means agreeing to the request. Maybe it's replacing parts up to a certain value. But if the staff member is really inclined to say no to a customer's request, you want someone higher on the chain of command to make that decision. It's a way of making certain that you're okay with saying no, all things considered. If you have a lot of trust in the experience and training of your staff, this may not be necessary.

To put things in perspective, the Ritz-Carlton Hotel had a policy for years where *any* employee could resolve an issue for any guest, costing up to $2,000.[4] You may think: *Well, if I had millionaires staying at my famous hotel, I'd do the same.* Maybe so, but think of the statement that policy makes for the Ritz: even a housekeeper has a lot of power to make things right for any customer, even the person who's staying only one night and does not appear to be wealthy.

This is all to give you food for thought. I'm not suggesting that you adopt any particular policy I've mentioned, but instead that you think really hard about how you can delight your customers in ways that mean there is no competition for what you offer. Maybe it's just a handwritten note on the first and fifth anniversaries of their first purchase with you. No doubt you and your staff can think of other things that you've experienced as customers, and how you might adapt those to your business. The possibilities are endless, and so is the upside to your business.

Where You Keep Customer Data

We've talked about the types of information that you should have, and the tremendous potential power it has to shoot customer loyalty to the moon. A more fundamental question is, Where do you keep your customer data?

There is a strong argument to be made that this is the most valuable asset you have in your business. Buildings and product inventory can be insured and replaced, but a list of customers—along with all their history and details—is much harder to replace. This is especially true if you have customers spread out all over the place, the way online businesses do.

If you have a system that contains it all, then that's great. If you have the equivalent of scraps of paper, a few spreadsheets, and whatnot, then you now have a high-priority problem to get fixed.

A fellow Deluxer, Cameron Potts, told me the story of his father, a small-business owner for the last 35 years of his career. Cameron's father, Don, owned a sheet metal business in Canada. Don was old school. He knew his customers extremely well and was friendly with all of them. He could remember their orders from years before, even down to the cost. Don would listen to their needs, sketch out a design, and hand it to his brother, Gord, who would make the item. That was their business and it made for a great living. But Don didn't have a computer and did all the invoices by hand. When the time came to retire, he *was* the business. There was no database to sell, no history to provide to a prospective buyer. That institutional knowledge was never kept anywhere other than his head.

Fortunately, keeping customer data need not be expensive. If you really cannot spend a dime at the moment, then use something like Google Sheets. It's a spreadsheet that is continuously backed up. You can store lots of information that way, and it is superior to storing precious customer data in some shoebox.

The next step up is a customer relationship manager (CRM). It also stores your data, but it can be made to do tricks, like every time you email customers any email replies from them can be automatically logged in the CRM. Some of these systems are free, and others are low cost—on the order of $25 per month for small businesses. One of Deluxe's close partners is Salesforce, which is one of the largest and best-known CRM companies in the world. They have CRMs for all sizes of business.

Testimonials

I've touched on this, but I want to drive home the point here. If you watch the *SBR* episodes, you'll notice a consistent pattern: many businesses didn't have a website before we did the makeover. If they in fact had one, it did not include many testimonials from customers. It is still hard to believe how some businesses still do not have websites, several decades after they came on the scene.

Another no-brainer way to increase your business is to *get and display more testimonials from satisfied customers.*

No business has a problem with *claiming* that it's good; everyone's website is positive. The problem businesses have is *proving* that they're good. Of course the very best proof is if you personally try a product or service and love it. The next-best proof is if a trusted friend loves it. Otherwise, you might look to *Consumer Reports* or some major newspaper that did a review and concluded that a business was best at whatever it does.

But what about everyone else? If you're a small business, you are unlikely to rank as the best in America for something. In that case, what do you do? How do you prove that you're great? The best way is to overwhelm people with lots of great testimonials.

First, let's take a store that sells fabrics and sewing supplies, and let's talk about what a great testimonial looks like.

- **It is specific.** People are not going to be persuaded if all the testimonial says is: "ABCD Sewing Center rocks!" A much stronger testimonial says, "ABCD Sewing Center is amazing. I've been a customer for 5 years and they are always friendly and helpful. Plus they have the best selection I've ever found."
- **It's believable.** That means that it is not ridiculously positive. You don't want this testimonial: "ABCD SEWING IS THE BEST ON THE PLANET!!!!! THEY MUST HAVE A MILLION FABRICS IN STOCK!!!!!!!" The best way to generate believability is to state a skeptical beginning. It sounds like this: "At first I had a hard time believing that a little store like ABCD Sewing could supply the fabrics I needed. But Alice was so helpful! If she didn't have it in stock, she found a way to get it."
- **If possible, you name names.** We all have seen testimonials that are positive, but end with "A.B." Well who is "A.B.," you ask? It's more believable to say "Archie Brooks, Fredonia NY." Even better is when you can match occupations. In other words, if you sell plumbing parts, then a strong testimonial ending would be "Mary O'Malley, Master Plumber License #12345, Alton, IL."

By the way, I'm not suggesting that you create testimonials. Absolutely not. That is unethical and could rightfully ruin your reputation. You should always use actual ones from customers. But what I am suggesting is that you can ask people to be specific, and talk about their skepticism before they bought. As I mentioned earlier, Deluxe provides a service called Reviews Promoter that helps small businesses to connect with their customers to solicit reviews. The best way to get a positive review is right after an interaction with a customer. Though it might seem pushy, customers who are satisfied with your service are usually not offended if you ask for a review. In fact, if a customer loved the service, that quick reminder is really all it takes to get someone online to make that quick review.

Another key task for you is to collect lots of testimonials. Many things in this world are gray areas, but this one is not: *you cannot overdo the collection of positive testimonials.* The more you have, the stronger the proof, and the further you pull away from your competitors who have a couple of testimonials, if that.

Think about how you size up a product or service. You hear all the claims and it seems like the solution you're after. Then you usually hear a lot of baloney about "world-class" and "amazing" and the stuff I mentioned earlier. Then you look for proof: How do I know it can do what it claims?

To answer that, consider Amazon, and take a category like "LED headlights." When I do that search, I literally see one manufacturer's headlights with 14 positive reviews. It is on the same page as another company's headlights, with 27,400 reviews. Literally. Now anybody can send a product to friends and relatives and generate 14 reviews. But *27 thousand?* And most of them are five-star reviews!

You don't need to shoot for 27,000 reviews, but you do need to shoot for a bunch. You want the reader to first be impressed with the volume; then you want her to wade into the reviews and kind of see herself in how they talk. Then you want her to reach a mental tipping point, where something snaps in a good way. It's like she concludes: *Okay, I'm done. Convinced. I'm going with this.*

So how many testimonials have you collected? None, you say? Well then, you're like your competition. Now's the time to start to collect them. Here's what you say to customers who've had a good experience:

Hey, I would be very grateful if you could please write a testimonial for me, if in fact you liked the product. It doesn't have to be long, and please just be truthful and as specific as you can. As you know, testimonials are so important and statements that come from customers are 10 times more valuable than anything I can say.

You can say words to that effect either in writing to someone or face-to-face.

Important tip: You want to get written approval from the testimonial giver. Yes, you're good friends now, and your buddy may have said some great things about you that you wrote down and put on your website. But friendships can take a hit when someone happens to look at your site and sees that she is quoted as saying something. That person may justifiably think: *Hey, they didn't even ask me if it was okay to quote me in public like that!*

Therefore, even for unsolicited testimonials, get approval in writing. Say: "Wow, thanks a ton for those nice comments you made the other day. Would it be okay if I quote you on that? This is what I'd like to say on my site: [Then you write out the testimonial]. Is that okay with you?"

If it's not okay, then you just dodged a bullet. But most likely your friend will say, "Oh sure! Go right ahead."

Awards and Other Recognition

Testimonials are a great form of social proof element, and so are awards and other recognition that you or your staff may have received.

Sometimes people forget about the honors they've received, and they may also be a bit modest about showcasing them. You can continue to be modest, but you're doing your leads and prospects a service by showing this information.

Businesses tend to sound the same about what they do, and that leaves visitors with the task of deciding who is experienced, helpful, trustworthy—or not so much. Therefore, make a list of all the things you can think of in the way of credentials:

- Suppliers have all sorts of classifications like: "Certified Installer," "Master Applicator," "Gold Level Partner," "Preferred Contractor," and so forth.
- You or your staff may have gone through training. Some possibilities: you could show certificates, name the number of hours completed, or explain that only 5 percent of technicians in the business ever get to a certain level of training or certification.
- If state licenses or other types of licensing apply to your business, say so. Some occupations have online databases with complaint histories and their resolutions. If you're in this sort of industry and have a clean record, say so.
- If you are part of the Better Business Bureau and have a good rating, then say so. If you've been a long-time member, that's important, too.

- Think creatively about what might be relevant. Let's say you do dog grooming and have an emergency medical technician certification. The EMT training had nothing to do with animals, but that's okay. It may still be a qualification in the eyes of customers that you have this sort of rigorous training for another type of creature.
- Earlier I discussed that a good way to get new business is to be part of local organizations like the Chamber of Commerce, a downtown association, and so on. But in this context it's also useful to list those memberships. It makes you not some out-of-towner but instead firmly a member of the community.
- It can be effective if you or your staff had previous jobs in relevant industries. Maybe your auto-body technician worked at a well-known paint manufacturer before joining your operation.
- If you support local charities and programs, it may be true that this is not a direct qualification for being in your line of business. Even so, I'd put it down. It means you're a good human being, and that can be important to other human beings.

Ultimately what you want is to have a sort of marketing-asset warehouse on your own business. It's where you keep all of your testimonials, awards, recognition, and any other proof elements you have collected. Then, depending on the type of marketing campaign you're creating, you can mix and match these elements and assemble a powerful message.

I go back to Brian Weavel of Anna's Pizza and Pasta in Winnebago, Illinois. Before he sold his business, Brian was a genius at promoting his work in the community and the awards he won. When they were named Best Pizza in the area, Brian shared the news on social media. When he was invited to judge a business contest at a local school, he shared it. If a celebrity came into town for pizza, he got a picture and shared that. Be proud and share your accomplishments; it helps to set your business apart.

~~~

Building relationships is about strengthening ties, as we discussed. It often involves putting your best foot forward with great testimonials, and so on. But what about that other foot? The one that needs some work? That's what we cover next.

9

Vulnerabilities

THE MILITARY AND intelligence communities have a concept called red teaming. It comes from when war-game scenarios are run. Let's say we were in the Cold War and we needed to know that we could counter a threat from the former Soviet Union. The U.S. military had red teams that were Americans who specialized in knowing everything about Soviet tactics. Their whole mission was to think like Soviets, dress like them, and use Soviet equipment, so when there was a war game, the red team's job was to defeat the American forces.

This concept has found its way into the business lexicon. When you red team your plans, you look for vulnerabilities in them. You ask, "What are we assuming? What could go wrong? Where are we most at risk?"

Maybe you have no active opponent working to thwart your plans. Even so, we all know about Murphy's Law, which says: "Anything that can go wrong, will go wrong." There is a hugely positive aspect to recognizing the negatives—the vulnerabilities—so you can plan around them.

This is exactly what the Deluxe team were focused on in Season 3, Episode 7, which was about Lighthouse Sounds. The owners, Jay Stanley and Alex St. Cin, worked hard to make Lighthouse a success. They contributed different things: Jay primarily was the money partner and Alex was the expert sound engineer.

Even though they were friends and partners, there was no written agreement between them about who owned and controlled what. It may seem awkward and even mildly rude for a business partner to announce one day that maybe there should be a written agreement between partners—but it has to happen. Any red team analysis should catch this vulnerability. As awkward as the discussion may be, it pales in comparison to the drama of sorting it out in court if things go south and finger-pointing begins.

Alex and Jay needed a written, legal agreement. Being friends is great, but they were running a business. They recognized the need to have an agreement because they both brought valuable assets to the table, so it wasn't a contentious issue.

Maybe you don't have the exact situation that Lighthouse faced, but think of what else might be out there: Has a relative loaned the business a lot of money with a certain understanding of how and when it will be repaid? Is an employee so knowledgeable about your special way of doing business that the person could set up shop as your competitor next month? Does one person literally have all the bank and computer log-in codes such that the place could collapse if this person suddenly were not in the picture?

These may all be painful scenarios to contemplate. They may be an insult to the goodwill you've worked so hard to develop. But this is another grown-up moment: you're running a business now. You don't have the luxury of doing only the planning that makes you feel warm and cozy. As a business owner, you must do the planning that sends a chill up your spine. It's the best way to anticipate and avoid much more chilling outcomes.

Your Physical Locations

We've seen in SBR that businesses run the gamut in terms of their physical circumstances. Some have cavernous spaces that can be an asset or liability, depending on how you look at it. If the business is paying for a lot of space that is not generating sales, that's a problem. Then again, a lot of space allows for future expansion. The sweet spot is to have enough space to grow, but not so much that it actually inhibits profitability.

We've also seen situations where the premises were not up to code. That might relate to how a kitchen is configured, or how an area has electricity in close proximity to water. There may be roof or entryway problems.

It's a human survival mechanism that allows us to get accustomed to situations where newcomers might gasp. Could anything like that be the case with your facility?

Obviously it would be great if Deluxe could swoop in and fix all these things. Then again, you may recall that in some cases, the issues were larger than even the *SBR* series was prepared to address.

That was the case in Season 4, Episode 6, with the Zion Climbing Center. I remember when Ty Pennington first stepped into Zion. People loved both coming to Zion and the folks who ran it, but it was housed in a dilapidated building that would have required our entire budget to fix. Ty was an eternal optimist and loved a challenge, but even he shook his head, wondering how we could fix the building. Whether you're part of *SBR* or not, in a sense the same process applies to prioritizing what must get addressed, and what must wait.

To that end, do what you can to list the issue, its priority, and what you know about the financial implications. For example, if you're paying for space you don't currently use, list the portion of rent that's effectively going to waste at the moment. If the issue is an overdue repair, list what you know of the cost. If you have no idea at all about the cost—and maybe that's why it's an overdue problem—then put that down as a current challenge.

We saw the opposite case at work in *SBR*, where a barber shop, auto detailer, and yoga center could all use more space. This is another case of no fancy math being necessary—but the math should be done about what expansion could mean.

In Chapter 3 we discussed how a simple spreadsheet can save lots of time in doing what-if analysis of different scenarios. Maybe this is my inner nerd talking, but I'm here to say that getting the hang of doing simple spreadsheet analysis will allow you to sleep better at night. The spreadsheet can handle all kinds of questions to guide your growth and plan against the downside. You can ask things like:

- What is the most we can pay for the additional space if we don't hire additional staff?
- If we buy the building instead of rent it, how many years will it be until we pay it off, using our average historical revenue and expense numbers?
- What are different mixes of products and services that could happen in order to pay for that space?
- Could we take advantage of it with current staff?

For example, at Nyce & Clean Auto Detailing in Season 5, Episode 1, Mike Plaza could use a spreadsheet to create scenarios:

#1: I'll do more detailing jobs in the new space, which I can do with current staff.

#2: I would use that space for window tinting only, and will need additional equipment and maybe staff.

#3: I'll use that extra space for window tinting, but maybe I could avoid buying the expensive equipment for now, and just buy the film custom printed for me. That's a higher cost per car for me, but a lower cost of equipment. This could enable me to see if the tinting service works for me before I commit to buying gear.

The other benefit of doing spreadsheet analysis is, for example, if you want to get financing for part of your future plans. You can only help your case when pitching it to a bank or money partner if you have spreadsheets that show what will happen under best-case, worst-case, and average scenarios.

Business Risks

You may not need a spreadsheet to identify some significant business risks, but you do need to write them down. Always write down your risks or concerns. This will force you to look at them with clear eyes. It is easy to simply psychologically look away. If it's on paper, you can't just look away. Writing down issues is a great discipline.

We saw just this type of risk with Lovett's in Season 3, Episode 5. Deluxe was about to invest significant money into the physical space of the restaurant, and it became known that the lease was month-to-month. In other words, the landlord could wake up one day, decide to sell the building, and give Lovett's a very short notice to clear out.

Even if Deluxe were not involved in the renovation, this is the sort of risk that businesses must identify when planning their growth. Where can the rug be pulled out from underneath you?

You might identify this kind of risk with your lease, but it may exist elsewhere, too. For example, do you have an exclusive-territory deal with a supplier that may expire soon? Perhaps you have locked in preferred pricing for something, and that's only good through the end of the year. Have you been pinning your hopes on a downtown revitalization project, but it's still in the planning stages and may not happen for a long time, if at all?

Another challenge with Lovett's was the fact that it was housed in an old drugstore that had an old-fashioned soda fountain. The owners of Lovett's and indeed many people in town wanted Deluxe to help pay to get the soda fountain working again. On the surface, it was a great idea—another revenue stream for Lovett's and a nod to the great past of Alton. But given that not many soda fountains exist today, the cost was prohibitive. Again, our entire budget could have gone to that one fix. Where was the most benefit? It was in other parts of their business.

This comes back to the "accurate thought" principle I brought up in Chapter 2. Some people may think: *I don't like this sort of planning. It's too negative. I'm a positive sort of person and I find ways to overcome difficulties.*

Well, in one sense, more power to you. It's great that you find a way around obstacles, but what is not good is when you avoid "this sort of planning" in an effort to stay positive, and, more importantly, greatly improves the odds of your success. There is an old saying, "if you fail to plan, you plan to fail."

Your Competition

We just finished a section in which I strongly advised you to think deeply about vulnerabilities in your business. Perhaps my timing could be better, but I'm going to ask you to do more planning that is not exactly fun.

This time, we're focused on the competition. This is another area where business owners will say things like, "Look, I'm focused on making my business as good as it can be. That means I'm not preoccupied with what my competitors are doing. Instead, I want them sweating about what I'm doing!"

It's fine to direct *almost all* of your attention to how you are growing your own business. I say "almost all" because it's a mistake to not know what your competitors are up to, and it's also sometimes a cop-out.

Let's face it: looking at what your competitors say and do is not a comfortable activity. They may even explicitly name you as a competitor in materials and explain how they're superior, which may make your blood boil because you know that they're twisting the facts, or you simply disagree with their assessment. But ignore your competitors at your own peril.

A common mistake many small business owners make is discounting their competitors as inferior, or artificially believing in their own superiority. This is a serious and sometimes fatal mistake. A competitor with a successful business is successful for a reason. Why?

Maybe your products or services are in fact superior, or at least every bit as good, so in that case, why spend even a second to focus on your competition? Wouldn't it be better to focus on your customers?

If you're going to grow your business, you need to be able to walk and chew gum at the same time. That means focusing on your own products and services, plus on your customers, plus on your competition, and so on.

My guess is you have some customers who are 100 percent faithful to you. They're more than customers—they're good friends—and they'd never in a million years go elsewhere. That's great. But this group of customers cannot possibly represent all or even most of your entire group of customers. In true 80/20 fashion, I'd guess they're the 10 percent or so that represent maybe 40 percent of your revenues.

The reality is that many of your customers are quite aware of what your competition is up to. That's not being disloyal; they're just being smart consumers.

Think of your own way you buy stuff. Let's think about you as a customer who needs new windows for your house. You search around and listen to what several companies say about how they're the best choice when, for example, replacing the windows. It's a big expense, and you really are overdue for new windows, so you do your homework.

Acme Windows has some amazing prices, but Window World talks about how vinyl is superior to wood that rots. Then again, Ajax Windows says that fiberglass windows are superior to lousy vinyl or wood, because fiberglass is more rigid and shrinks less.

As a consumer, you're no expert! You just want decent windows at a decent price, and you don't want to think of them for another 15 years after you get the replacements. Again as a consumer, you will encounter one of two situations. The first is that every window company talks in a vacuum about how its stuff is superior. Now you have to figure it all out for yourself.

The second situation is a competitor who says, "We know you have choices of window installers. We know there are lots of window types and choosing among them can get really confusing. Here is a guide that honestly shows the pluses and minuses of each type of window. We think we have great windows, but they're not the right solution for every type of consumer." If you heard that, which company would you choose? Me too.

Almost all companies are "me" focused, and only a handful look at things from the customer's perspective. The businesses that operate from the customer's perspective are usually the most successful.

That means that you should have a solid understanding of what your competitors offer, and, if they're smart, they'll be doing the same with respect to you. If there are aspects of your competitors' offerings that are indeed superior to yours, you need to know that. You may still choose not to change anything, but at least you'll be doing so with your eyes open. Then again, you may be in a position where you could make improvements that meet or beat what the competition offers.

Remember that sometimes competitors can actually help each other. Let's say you sell swimming pools and someone calls you to ask if you sell in-ground pools. You explain that you do not, but you can give them the name of a great in-ground pool installer. You could have a relationship with that installer. After all, sometimes the above-ground guy will get a customer who balks at the cost of an in-ground pool. In that case one company refers prospects to the other company that also does a good job. They might have a financial relationship, or they could just agree to refer appropriate clients to each other.

Think about what just happened. You referred a customer to another company, instead of pretending that you could be all things to all people. Even if the customer goes to the competitor you referred her to, she will have a positive impression of you. She might very well be chatting with her friends, and one of them now wants a pool. The friend might not have the cash to go with the in-ground pool company, but she's heard good things about you and ends up being your customer.

The same co-referral relationship could exist between companies in the same industry, where one company tends to do much larger jobs than the other, or they service different territories.

I'm all about the abundance mentality and not the zero-sum game. The concept of "zero sum" is that whatever is gained by one side is lost by the other. To me, that's how losers think. The abundance mentality is that there is an ocean of customers, and if I dip my cup or bucket or tanker truck into the ocean, the water level does not change for someone else who wants to dip in. If we're doing a good job and helping customers, then we'll see the fruits of our labors.

~~~

We just have covered a number of areas that deserve attention, because they can be weak links in the chain that is your business. The next chapter covers what is absolutely a weak or nonexistent link in most businesses—but it has the potential to grow your business like few other activities can.

10

The Power of Email

A Few Years before W.R. Hotchkiss had the idea of creating the Deluxe Corporation, a famous story went viral. That's right—even in the 1800s, news could spread about something that captured people's imagination.

The story was about a farmer named Ali Hafed, who lived in what is now called the Middle East, and who was quite wealthy by ancient standards. He was content with his substantial orchards, grain fields, and gardens, among other wealth. One day a traveler passed through his land and Ali welcomed him to stop. The traveler was an old priest, and he told the farmer a story about diamonds. Of course Ali knew about diamonds, but the way the traveler spoke about them captivated him. Ali was told that in some parts of the world, diamonds as big as your thumb were known to exist, and were strewn about for anyone to find.

That night Ali couldn't sleep, and the next day he was discontented with the thought of the real wealth he could have, if he just found a single big diamond. Long story short, Ali sold his farm and went on a quest to find real wealth in the form of diamonds. He traveled the world and after a while his money was gone. Completely dejected, Ali threw himself into the ocean.

Some years later the old priest came through the same land where Ali welcomed him all those years ago. This time he was welcomed by the current land owner. As they were sitting, the traveler noticed a rock on the fireplace mantel. He looked at it and said: "This is a diamond! I told Ali Hafed about them! Has he returned?" The current farmer said "Oh that? It's no diamond. It's just a pretty rock we found in our garden."

They went outside and soon found several more like it, and sure enough they were diamonds. Thus began the Golconda Diamond Mine, and it was to become the most famous on earth. The story became known as "Acres of Diamonds."[1]

What Are You Sitting On?

As odd as it may seem, the chances are excellent that right now, you are sitting on a form of wealth that you've heard something about but have dismissed. I'm talking about email marketing.

You've vaguely concluded that it's either outdated, spammy, not applicable to your business, or all of the above. Let's see about that.

"Email is spammy."

We all have scars from our experiences with email. These days, spam filters have become extremely good at separating the junk from emails we want to read. Even so, we all know someone who clicked on a legitimate-looking email only to have the computer become infected with malware.

It would be a mistake to label the whole category of email as spam. When done correctly, email is one of the best examples of permission marketing:

- Your favorite store for outdoor clothing has had a hard time keeping in stock the sweater you want, so *you've asked them* to notify you as soon as your size is available.
- The alumni directory from your school has a place where you can list your email, so *you gave them* your address. Every now and then you'll get an email from a classmate.

- The people who are offering that Zoom call about parenting will send the webinar details to you via email, which integrates with the calendar you *gave them access to*, so all the details are in both places.

Modern email tools are now quite sophisticated. In addition to the effective spam filter, you can choose to have your emails sorted by type—social media, promotions, and so on. You can also set up custom actions so particularly important emails from your spouse, boss, or sports buddy can be highlighted, forwarded, and so on. In short, email has grown up from a single spammy bucket to a legitimate, sophisticated channel for receiving information that you've specifically asked for.

"Email marketing is so yesterday. The world has moved on."

It's true that email has been around for longer than social media, but I have to ask: Have you actually deleted all of your email accounts and only communicate with people via social media these days?

I'm guessing not. When you get a car loan or a home mortgage, does the lender ask for your Facebook address in order to send you important documents or updates? Despite the never-ending effort to improve spam filters, email remains the most important and official online method of getting in touch with people.

"I can write, but I'm not a writer."

You don't need to be a professional writer to pull this off. You just need to be yourself. I'm not suggesting that you have any different an approach from how you speak with people in real life or on social media. Write the way you talk, and in the style that people know you for.

"My customers are on social media."

Your customers may very well be on social media, but that's not the point. What I'm trying to do is get you more business. I don't suggest that you stop doing social media, but instead that you start to do more email marketing, because your customers are also on email.

It's not an either/or question; instead, good business is a both/and proposition. Part of strengthening your brand is making sure you're seen in more places, like in the email inboxes of your customers. However, the most effective email marketing follows a specific procedure, and most businesses have no clue about this. More about this later.

I'll give you two other super-important reasons why you need to be doing more email, even if your customers love social media:

First, you're in control of your message. Let's say 50 customers have given you their email addresses because you told them that you'll send them a guide to keeping their vehicle exteriors in good shape during each season. If you send them four helpful emails, spread out across a year, then cool. You delivered on your promise and you've strengthened the relationship with those customers.

Contrast that with social media: Did you know that when you decide to follow someone on social media, you may or may not see all the stuff that person posts? You don't get to decide what you'll see from that person—the social-media platform decides for you. Maybe you'll see it all, and maybe you won't. You shouldn't have to run your business in the hope that your messages get through someone's news algorithm. You deserve to have your messages delivered, period, and that's what email will do for you.

The second critical factor relates to getting found in search engines like Google. Let's say you write up those helpful articles about maintaining your vehicle in all seasons. If that's only posted on social media, you don't have exclusive rights to that content; the platform has a license to use it.

Don't you want to get full credit for your effort? If so, then send an email with an announcement about the most recent article, and direct customers from your email to your site, where you put the article. Google will now index that article and you will get a little incremental credit for this material when your customers visit your site. In other words, if the content is good enough, Google will take notice and will rank your article in its results when someone googles that topic.

You can also go to social media and tell people that you have the article, and that's fine. The difference is that the article now lives on your site, and not on some platform you don't own.

Yet Another Key Reason for You to Take Email Marketing Seriously

That reason is because your competition most likely is not taking it seriously. They're thinking about all the same objections we just covered; they haven't read what you just did about why you should be doing email marketing, so this is one more opportunity to distance yourself from that competition. Deluxe has been working with businesses for more than a century and although email marketing has only been around for about 20 years, we saw time and again that businesses ignored this tool.

When to Use Email Marketing for Maximum Effect

We just covered the "why" about email marketing. Let's now talk about when to do it, and then we'll hit the topic of how to do it easily and effectively.

Major Use #1 for Email: Name Capture

In Chapter 8 I discussed how relationships can be cultivated through the capture of your online visitors' names. I want to make some additional important points here.

As I said earlier, it's not enough to have a box on your website saying "Sign up to be on our mailing list." That is giving nothing of value at all. Why should I want to be on your mailing list? It's much better to do the following:

1. **Change the language on the button.** People don't generally like to sign up for anything because it sounds like a commitment. You might try saying "Leave your information" or "Register here." Words matter.
2. **Give them *multiple* reasons to get on your list.** People regard their contact information to be valuable, as they should. It's important to give something of value in exchange for that information. Here are examples of reasons to leave their name:
   - "Be notified of all our specials before most people find out about them."

- "Get a special surprise on your birthday."
- "Be the first to know about our closeouts."
- "Find out when we introduce a new flavor."
- "Hear when we drop another how-to video."
- "We'll send a coupon for a free sample."
- "You'll be invited to exclusive, private events for our best customers."

You get the idea. Come up with several reasons, if possible, so they conclude that getting on your list is a no-brainer. In the case of *SBR*, we send out a newsletter to our subscribers. The idea isn't to sell anything, but to give our followers a sneak peak into the series; for instance, how the filming is coming, a behind-the-scenes look, or a teaser from one of our hosts.

At Deluxe, we use our email list to share information about coming new products or to announce major news. In this way, we are building a relationship with our customers, and keeping them engaged with us. While any single email may not yield a sale, the collection of emails reminds the customer of their valued relationship with us, and at some point in the future that strong relationship turns into a sale. It's about building relationship, as described in Chapter 9.

3. **Give them confidence to continue.** Tell them how they can easily unsubscribe and how you'll never spam them or sell their name.

Here's a big red warning about capturing contact information on your website for later emailing: do not ask for too much information! It's a temptation to ask for all the information that *you'd like to know*. But remember that people are rightfully concerned about getting spammed, and they will not give lots of information without a solid reason to do so.

You usually will see this problem crop up on sites where they ask for a phone number, especially for a mobile phone. As a consumer, when I see that I think *there's no way I'm giving you my cell, only to have you call me day and night. Plus you'll probably sell it.* Not only do I leave that part blank, but I often just abandon the whole form without leaving any information. They went too far.

The better approach is first to ask for the minimum, like email and first name. Then as you cultivate a relationship with people in your store or online, you can ask for further information and add that to their record. It's a little bit like dating, where you need to take it nice and slow, and look for signs that the other person is genuinely interested. Plus, you only have a few seconds to grab their attention. If you ask for too much information, chances are they will just give up and move on to something else.

Major Use #2 for Email: Segmentation

One of the great benefits of small businesses over giant ones is the personal relationship and attention that small businesses can bring to the table. The barista at the corner coffee shop begins to make your large iced coffee, 5-pump vanilla 10-pump hazelnut with a splash of soy as soon as you walk in the door. The veterinarian knows your dogs by name and how they like to be handled. Contrast this with some of the giant corporations that you've been with for 25 years, yet their letters address you as: "Dear Cable Customer."

This is where small can run circles around big: use the power of email to speak more directly to your customer. As you know, people have strong preferences. For example, if you are an avid collector of dolls, you either are a "boxer" who keeps the dolls in the box or an "unboxer" who takes them out. The boxers think the unboxers are trash, because they're ruining the collecting value by taking the dolls out of the box. The unboxers think the boxers are crazy for not enjoying the dolls outside of their cases.

Now imagine that you own a store that sells dolls. You could have something on your site that asks people to leave their contact information, and whether they would like to receive updates on:

- Unboxed dolls
- Boxed dolls
- Other (specify)

Now when you email customers, you can write a special note to just the unboxers, talking about how great it is to take those dolls out and get maximum enjoyment. Your email to the boxers would appeal to their own philosophy.

You may think that the boxer/unboxer example is extreme, but in reality we do this with everything! People shop at the same supermarket, but one group is on a keto diet with loads of meat; another group eats just about anything; and still others are vegetarians, vegans, gluten-free, and so on.

In my experience, people don't realize the possibilities for segmentation within their business. If you own a fishing-tackle shop, you might think that all your customers like to fish. Yes, that's true, but their segments might be people who fish exclusively for bass. Even within bass, there are distinctions where I might think of myself as a small-mouth bass specialist (that really is a thing) versus all those large-mouth bass people. I might distinguish myself as only using artificial lures to catch my fish, when other people use worms and other bait.

Dig into *any* area and you will find distinctions and segments that people in that area find important. Whatever the business, this holds true: if you own a cycle shop, then there may be the folks who have carbon-fiber bikes, or the fat-tire enthusiasts, or even the people who like to have no speeds and no brakes on their bikes (I kid you not). If you speak just to one of these groups at a time, it's so much more powerful than speaking to bike owners in general.

It's fine to have one mailing list for all of these people, but my point is this: if you segment them into their stated preferences, your message will resonate that much more. When you narrow the group, you can deepen the effect of the message.

Another Way to Segment

Most businesses don't bother with the segmentation just mentioned, and not even one business in a thousand thinks to do a different type of segmentation: by frequency.

The way this works is that every six months or so you send an email to your different segments saying something like:

I hope you're finding my emails to be helpful. However, I know that everyone's different, and I want to make sure that I am communicating with you with just the right frequency for your taste. Therefore, please check one of the boxes below:

- I could use somewhat fewer emails than you send me now.
- Your email frequency is just about right—keep 'em coming.
- If you have more emails to send me that are useful, please do so.
- Please just unsubscribe me.

Have you ever seen this? It's brilliant in how it does not assume that one size fits all. Besides, it's so respectful of customers that it's bound to leave a good impression.

Major Use #3 for Email: Automatic Relationship Building

I know what you're thinking: Huh? How can you build relationships automatically?

It's possible with email. In business it's called an "autoresponder sequence." Here's how it works.

Let's say you do car detailing and you've done proper segmentation on your list. By "proper" I mean you've taken the time to ask people if they'd like occasional information about subspecialties. They may be things like convertibles, vintage cars, muscle cars, Shelby Cobras, pickup trucks, and so on.

You gather this information and after a while you see that there are a number of people in the convertibles segment. You start to think about what information you could provide them over time. What do you know about convertibles and detailing? Maybe there are some chemicals that will quickly ruin a convertible top. Or perhaps the way to clean a cotton-fabric top is very different from how a synthetic top should be cleaned.

Think about these topics, and pay special attention to the questions you've gotten over the years about them, the myths and misconceptions people have, and the best practices you've learned.

Now you're in a position to write a series of helpful emails, driving people to articles on your site. Each email is on a subtopic relating to convertibles, and each one drives people to a brief (or long) article on

> **Pro Tip**
>
> Use the language of the specialized area. Some people call them convertibles, but others will say "rag top" or "soft top." By using the language that insiders know, you telegraph that you're an insider.
>
> It's the same with just about everything. Outsiders know Minneapolis, where Deluxe headquarters are located, as Minneapolis. Often people will call it the Twin Cities. Some might call it the "612" because of the 612 area code, in the same way some in Denver say 5280, referring to feet above sea level as the "mile-high" city. Knowing the local language, nicknames, and slang gives you an inside track.

your site. Maybe sometimes you have a quick bit of advice, in which case just have it all in your email.

Pretty soon you'll have assembled a series of emails on the topic of convertibles. Now you can go to your ESP (more on this later in the chapter) and load in all those emails. You then specify that you want the first one to go out the moment someone fills out the form; then you may have the second email go out a week later, and the third a week after that.

Really smart businesses have long sequences of email content that they add to, when they think of a new thing to talk about. They also will have content sequences like this for each of the specialties. In our example, maybe the convertible sequence has seven emails, and eventually the Shelby Cobra has 11 emails.

Once you have this set up, it just runs automatically for you, for each new person who filled out your form. You're providing value about the special thing they love to deal with. It's no wonder, then, that when you occasionally write to them to say you have a special event or discount, you'll be regarded not as a nuisance spammer, but instead a welcome friend in their inbox.

Grown-Up Moment

Most people reading this book will not do this work of using email fully and effectively. Then again, most people get the results that most people get. In this book I'm showing you ways to break out of your hamster wheel of endless work for not much progress. In order to do that, it's necessary to take some steps that most people will not bother to do. This stuff does not even cost much money; you can write emails during slow times in the business, or while you're in some waiting room, using odd scraps of time. Sending emails is extremely low cost and often is free, so it's not a matter of money, or of special talent, or even of time. It's a matter of the will to get it done.

The Mechanics of Good Email Marketing

I've talked about why email marketing is so important, and when to use it. Now let's discuss how to put it into practice with a minimum of cost and effort.

"I don't want to give out my personal email to anyone; that's a prescription for even more spam."

You're right. You should not give out your personal email. In fact, even if you didn't care about spam, you shouldn't give out that email. Why? Because which of the following email addresses looks more professional if your business is Acme Auto Parts?

- crazyvikingsfan4eva@yahoo.com
- support@acmeautoparts.com

Part of your brand should be an email address that conveys a professional image, and is easy to say and spell. That means no substitutions like "u" for "you" and "4" when you mean "for."

By the way, it's very easy for you to get different email addresses for your business. Once you have a domain name, your website-builder person can easily create as many email addresses as you need. You'll be able to have single-purpose email addresses that help to keep things organized. For example, orders@acmeautoparts.com can go to one person automatically, and service@acmeautoparts.com can be routed to someone else.

You Need an ESP

Just as you have an Internet service provider that gives you the ability to get on the Internet at your business or home, you need an email service provider, or ESP, when you have a business.

Your personal email account is not the same as an ESP. Google, Microsoft Outlook, and AOL are examples of services used by individuals. The problem is that those services will not allow you to send an identical email to lots of your customers at one time. These companies know the content of your emails and if they detect that you're blasting the same message to hundreds or even just a few dozen people at one time, they'll freeze your account. It's a violation of all those tiny paragraphs of legal terms that you agreed to when you signed up.

Instead, what you need to do is open an account with a service like Aplus.net and many others. These companies specialize in providing email services to businesses of all sizes. Here are some of the benefits of having an ESP:

- **They allow you to send the same email to lots of people at once.** This action, which will get your personal email account frozen, is no problem at all with the ESPs.
- **You can easily tie in a form on your site** to the ESP so when people give their contact information, it automatically goes into the system. Zero manual labor.
- **They automatically handle stuff like people wanting to unsubscribe.** This is important because the law requires businesses to make it fast and easy to unsubscribe.
- **They'll give you statistics** about how many of your emails were delivered, how many people opened them, whether anyone clicked on links you had in the email, and many other measurements.

- **They'll save you time and make you look more professional.** These services have lots of predesigned, professional-looking templates for emails. Instead of having big blobs of text that don't welcome the reader, your emails can look inviting.
- **Your email is more likely to be delivered.** As we've discussed, spam filters are highly sensitive and effective these days. But having tough spam filters also means it's sometimes a challenge for legitimate mail to get delivered. When you send your email through an ESP, they'll help to guide you on what seemingly innocent language in your email could get you in trouble and how to avoid that.
- **They'll help to keep you out of trouble in other ways.** The ESPs have systems that automatically put the correct disclosures on emails you send out. Those disclosures are required by the federal government.
- **Here's additional good news: getting an ESP is very inexpensive.** Some ESPs will give you a free account if you're only sending to a few hundred people. Even if you have a few thousand, the cost is usually very low, and you don't need to be locked into any long contract.

~~~

By now I hope you see how email has the power to significantly deepen relationships with your prospects and customers at a very low cost. Fortunately, as business owners we get to use multiple methods to attract and keep customers. Yet another great method is the topic of the next chapter.

11

The Right Way to Use Social Media

For Such A relatively young technology, social media certainly has generated more than its share of myths and misconceptions. Given how very important social media is to small businesses, it's worth looking closely at how best to harness this tool for your benefit.

Social Media Myths and Realities

In almost every episode of *SBR*, we've seen businesses that benefited from having a much more robust social-media presence. At the same time, I realize that you are most likely extremely short on time and resources, so you need to be convinced that spending time on something needs to have a significant chance of making a difference in your bottom line. Let's therefore look at the elephant in the room—the common opinions about social media—before we spend any time talking about how to use it in a business setting.

"My customers are not on social media."

A variation of this objection is for someone to say, "My customers are mostly on Facebook; it's a waste of time to use LinkedIn because they don't use it." Exactly how do you know that? Doing a broad and comprehensive survey would be one way. Then again, there is a well-known phenomenon of people telling pollsters and surveys one thing, and acting differently.

The thing about social media is that people confuse what gets all the attention by the news media with what the tool can be used for. In other words, on any given day we might hear about some Twitter war of words between politicians; or it could be the latest boy band out of South Korea; or some other distracting, shallow event. The actual social-media platforms are much more than that stuff, as we discuss in a moment.

The only authoritative way to say whether your customers are on social media is to use different social-media platforms in order to find out. You don't need to spend millions or even thousands of dollars, but instead just hundreds of dollars to advertise on social-media sites and see if your target market responds to those ads.

Facebook allows people with just about any specific interest under the sun to create groups that are tightly controlled by the person who created the group, in terms of who is allowed in the group. There are public groups, where anyone can join, and private groups, where people can apply to be accepted. There are even secret groups, where you need an invitation to be considered for membership and the group is not listed anywhere.[1]

Sites like Facebook, LinkedIn, Pinterest, and others have become extraordinarily sophisticated in the data they collect on users. In the case of Facebook it ranges from 98 data points[2] to 52,000 data points per individual,[3] depending on whom you believe. Either way, all that data allows a social-media platform to serve up highly targeted ads to specific audiences.

When you're setting up an ad in Facebook, you can get very specific about the types of people who should be shown your ad. In fact, you can upload a list of your actual clients and tell Facebook to show your ads to other people who closely match your clients. Those other people are called "lookalike audiences." After you run those ads for a little while, you'll know what sort of results you're getting. Just be careful to not reach premature conclusions after a day or two, as I discussed in Chapter 1. Try different channels in a methodical fashion in order to know which ones yield the best results for you.

You can also determine where your business is best seen. For instance, Nooma yoga has a massive following on Instagram. The visual nature of their business lends itself to Instagram, where they can post short videos, photos, inspirational quotes, and upcoming classes. Casey Cox, the owner, did her research and her mostly female, young clientele *live* on Instagram. Although Casey ensures that she has a Facebook, Twitter, Pinterest, and LinkedIn account for Nooma as well, Instagram is where she spends most of her time.

"Social media is not a serious media channel. After all, we have people posting what they ate for lunch, and doing pouty-lip selfies."

It's a mistake to regard social media as just a trivial, juvenile meeting place. Instead, social media has been around long enough that it has grown into a whole ecosystem of areas where people connect for specialized purposes. Social media has incredible power to influence elections, so of course it has influence over products consumers buy or where they shop.

Certainly it's true that a lot of the posts you see in the media are the shallow tweets of celebrities and others. There are also plenty of examples of junk being posted and discussed. However, to say that "social media is not serious" is like saying "apartments are a cheap way to live" when some apartments rent for $36,000 per month.[4]

The key is to get specific. If you're an indoor rock-climbing operation in Abilene, Texas, you can post photos and articles that have to do with indoor rock climbing. You can include hashtags like "#AbileneRockClimbing," and that will help people who search for "Abilene Rock Climbing" to find you.

You can also advertise on Google and other sites. For example, it's possible to have your ads on social media only show when someone lives within 40 miles of Abilene and has expressed some interest at some point concerning indoor rock climbing.

"I hate social media, and it's painful for me to use it."

Fortunately, you do not have to use social media personally in order to benefit from it. The media channel has become so widespread that there is a good chance that some relative of yours—perhaps a relatively young person who was born with a smartphone—could help you out here. You can also hire someone for a few dollars on Fiverr, as I discussed before.

It really is a good idea to get someone to help you if you truly spend no time on social media. It's a bit like regional mannerisms with a given language. For example, in the South you'll hear the term "y'all" but if you're a Northerner, you may not realize that it's a big no-no to say "y'all" when speaking to one other person. It's only used when speaking to more than one person, or else it sounds weird. You need to find someone who's thoroughly immersed in whichever social-media platform you choose to be on.

So Many Platforms, So Little Time

It is a mistake for a business owner to think *I don't do things halfway, so I want to be on all of the platforms like Facebook, Twitter, Pinterest, TikTok, Clubhouse, and whatever else is out there.*

That's a bad idea for two reasons. First, it's impossible. There are hundreds of social-media sites, so you'll never be done. Second, you'll never keep them updated if you must publish to a bunch of them. What's worse than not having a social-media presence is having a stale one, with the last post from a year ago. That conveys the message that either you don't care, you're out of business, or both.

It's much better to start on one or two platforms. Let's take a quick look at the main ones:

- **Facebook** is, of course, the most famous social-media platform. As an individual or as a business, you can have a "page" where you talk about who you are and what you do.
- **LinkedIn** is known as being more of a place where professionals go to discuss business or look for jobs, or for candidates to fill a job.

- **YouTube** is an odd hybrid. It's the world's second-largest search engine behind Google,[5] but it also has the ability for people to comment on videos, like or dislike them, and share them with others. If you have videos longer than two or three minutes, YouTube is probably the best place to show them, because people there are accustomed to longer videos.
- **Instagram** is very image-oriented. It's possible to post both photos and videos, and to advertise on this platform.
- **Pinterest** is also highly image-oriented, with users collecting and sharing "pins" or cards that have images or videos on them. Many pins have a "how-to" theme relating to recipes, how to dress well, interesting interior design ideas, and so on. Each pin can link back to your website if you wish.
- **Twitter** is all about instant commentary. You don't post photos on Twitter, but your short messages instantly go out to your followers.

Countless other, smaller platforms exist, but we recommend that you start with even just one of the most well known and popular from the list above. In fact, if you could only have one social-media platform, it should be Facebook, just based on its sheer size and flexibility. It's the big dog in the social-media space, the way Google dwarfs the many other search engines.

As I stated earlier, it is good to be active on many channels, but also to find your audience. Nooma is focused on a younger, female base and Instagram plays well to that base, as does TikTok and Clubhouse. Though still relatively new, Facebook is no longer considered young and hip, so you are reaching a more mature audience with it. LinkedIn is focused on business professionals. Knowing where your audience is located is critical.

Even though a certain social-media platform may seem tailor-made for your business, you really can get creative about posting to others and making it work. For example, if you're a tattoo parlor, it's a no-brainer to be on Instagram and probably Pinterest. But if that tattoo parlor is going for maximum social-media exposure, it could do a professional LinkedIn article about the economics of tattoo parlors in COVID times.

The Thing About Twitter

Just as I recommend that you start with Facebook, I suggest you avoid Twitter unless you have specialized needs. The reason is that there's something about Twitter that brings out the worst in people. We've all seen celebrities, sports legends, and politicians get into serious trouble with the tweets that they decide to dash off in the middle of the night. Someone says something dumb or that can be misunderstood, and then someone else's gloves come off. Now there's a fight breaking out and that generates viral sharing of the nastiness. It's endless.

Here's another problem: Twitter does not allow you to edit a post once you've sent it, even if it was a 100 percent error that someone made from cutting and pasting the wrong text about something that has nothing to do with your business. You can retract a post entirely, but even that is something that then becomes the subject of a journalist sniffing around and discovering that you deleted a tweet: *Why did they delete the tweet? Hmm, maybe there's a story here. . . .*

Even though I would avoid Twitter for these reasons, I said it could work if you have a "specialized need." Let's say you run a taco truck. There is no better mechanism for you to get business than to have a Twitter account. You can say, "Hey, we'll be on the corner of Atlantic Avenue and Main Street at noon! Stop by for our famous Double Taco Bunk Bed!"

The same kind of instant messaging to large groups will be great if you run a nonprofit and are holding a food drive or other community event. Twitter can't be beat for such things.

There's one other great use for Twitter, and that is to keep an eye open for your brand showing up. This has become a thing, where, for example, someone will have a horrible experience on an airplane and will then tweet the experience to the world, together with stuff like #nightmare #terribleservice #willneveruseagain.

As you may know, hashtags like "#nightmare" are social media's way of categorizing and bringing attention to things. You should be monitoring your brand and any often-used names for your business so that you can catch bad tweets early and respond to them. In the airplane case, if an airline did not respond to a tweet, then some people may wonder if the airline is guilty. At the very least they may wonder whether the airline is aware of what customers think. Or, worse, does it not even care to reply? All are bad outcomes of not monitoring Twitter and not responding appropriately.

How Do I Determine Which Social-Media Platforms I Should Start With?

The way to determine other platforms to use in addition to Facebook is to figure out where your target customers are spending the most time. Notice I say "target customers" and where they spend "the most" time. If you're a business of any size, you probably have some customers who like to use all sorts of platforms, so it's important to focus your effort on your bread-and-butter customers.

Assuming that you know that customer profile, you can do three things to identify where they may be spending the most time on social media:

1. **Ask them.** Don't assume that you know your customers; ask them. Say, "I'm thinking of focusing my efforts on certain social-media platforms. Do you have any favorites?" Be sure to ask one or two dozen people, so you don't draw the wrong conclusions from a couple of vocal people.
2. **Google them.** With literally billions of users, social-media platforms have a wealth of data on their user profiles. You can type in a term like "social media platform demographics" and you'll see many current reports. There you may learn, for example, that only 9 percent of 50- to 65-year-olds use Snapchat and three times that number of the same age group use Pinterest.[6]
3. **See where your competitors are active.** Perhaps your competitors do less than you do on social media; then again, some of them may use the channel heavily and successfully. I don't recommend that you plagiarize them, but instead get some inspiration from competitors. If one of them has a highly active presence on, say, Instagram, then you can do some detective work to see what sorts of images and videos they're posting, how often, what themes they use, and so on. That may give you ideas of how to craft your own messages.

How Often Should My Business Be Posting?

Here's a rule of thumb: whichever social-media platforms you choose to use, it's smart to post at least once per week at a minimum. That may or may not seem like a lot to you, but in the world of social media, that's by no means a highly active site.

With your social-media presence, you're trying to build a relationship and stay in the mind of the slice of your customers who enjoy social media. That may only be a third of your customer base, but to that third, they tend to be on social media a lot. Posting any less frequently than weekly will come across as being stale and inactive to them. In fact, if people look you up on social media and notice that your last update was five months ago, they may very well conclude that your business is closed. They may not call to confirm, but may just go to your competitor.

It's a good idea to get into the habit of posting anything unusual about your business operations on social media. For example, if your hours have changed or will be longer during the holidays, be sure to post that. Although it's true that Google will often grab business hours from your website, Google won't necessarily update that information as regularly as you can through social media. Besides, it's easier to blast out a quick message on social media than it is for most people to get parts of their websites updated. Other business operations to update via social media include if a road is closed near your business, or if you have your online shopping cart down for a little while for maintenance.

Again, I love to use Nooma as an example. Casey Cox and her team post several times a day and receive many dozens of likes and comments. Their followers crave the content and it's the right mix for them. A business like an Irish pub maybe doesn't need as many posts as an active yoga studio, but once you are online in this way, it is important to be consistent.

Remember, these posts or comments on social media do not have to be lengthy. Frequency matters much more than length.

What Tools Exist That Can Help Me with This Whole Area?

You're in luck. There is a robust collection of tools to make small businesses come across professionally, right from the get-go.

Let's assume that you're not a designer. You can use a tool like canva.com to look great. You can tell it what sort of typeface and brand colors you would like to use, and then it will combine those preferences with premade templates. For example, if you're looking to do a great Instagram Story, it will create something that's designed just for that sort of placement, versus what looks best for a LinkedIn Banner.

This is important because one size definitely does not fit all when it comes to social-media posts. Many platforms will refuse to show your post if it does not conform to specific design sizes and layouts. It's a huge relief to use a tool that keeps track of all those details so you or your social-media person can focus more on the message.

Canva.com and other tools usually have free accounts where a certain number of basic features are available, and they have paid levels in order to access all features. Usually even the paid levels are relatively inexpensive.

Another tool to consider is from sproutsocial.com.[7] It's not free, but then again it will save you or your social-media person a lot of effort. It allows you to load up a bunch of posts at one time and schedule them to go out when they're most likely to be well received. You can also configure the tool to make it easy to respond to people who post, comment, like, dislike, tweet, and whatever else they may do, related to your social-media presence.

This is important because even people who enjoy social media on a personal level will sometimes get overwhelmed. when it comes to using it for business. They're accustomed to posting things they feel like posting.

When businesses use social media, posting needs to be more organized and methodical because the repercussions on a post that goes bad are greater. Regular posts need to go out or else the social-media platforms will take notice and make your online presence less visible. To put it another way, when a fun pastime becomes a job, things sometimes must change. Having a tool that automates some of the work can make it seem less like work.

Finally, a good all-around resource for social-media advice is HubSpot.com. They have some extremely detailed blog posts and courses on not only social media, but just about every other online activity. They also have forums where anyone can ask even very specific questions and someone with an answer is likely to reply.

Be Careful About Photography

Here are several best practices for you to consider.

1. **Choose aspirational images that will appeal to your customer, not just to you.** This is hard for some business owners to grasp. Just because you like an image does not mean your target customers will see it similarly. Choose images that are most flattering, show your business in the most favorable light—literally—and make the customer feel good when they see it. The same plate of food can look awful or delicious depending on how the image is arranged and set up. Always ask customers for their thoughts on the images you plan to use—just be sure to offer multiple choices so you really hear the feedback. Most customers would love to share their opinion and will be flattered you asked.

2. **Be sure you have the rights to use an image.** Social media is a highly visual place, so—unless you're doing Twitter—you are going to need a steady supply of images. Services like Canva.com and UnSplash.com have whole libraries of images for you to use. Wherever you get your images, be careful to look at the ownership and rules associated with the images and don't just copy an image from somewhere and stick it in your post or on a website.

   Companies like Getty Images and Adobe Stock have many millions of images for sale. They are *for sale*. If you go to their sites or another similar one, and copy an image that you use in a post or web page, you may think, *How can they know that little old me used that image? They won't care. The Internet is way too big.*

   Wrong. They have ways of monitoring daily exactly who is using which image anywhere on the Internet. If you're lucky you will get a slap on the wrist. It's more likely that you will literally get an invoice for several hundred dollars, accompanied by a letter from their attorney. It's just not worth it to play this game.

   The same is true when you go to Google Images and look at the zillions of images there. If you look closely, they'll say "Images may be subject to copyright. Learn More." You should click the Learn More link and do just that.

3. **When you take a photo of someone, be sure to ask for permission to use it in social media.** You really do not want to get a phone call from someone who sees her image on Facebook on your business page who had no idea you took the photo. It may even be a nice photo, but that does not matter. The same rules apply to photographs of children.

The law is sometimes confusing when it comes to when people's images can be used and where. If you're doing a whole ad campaign and use someone's photo, you better have a signed "model release." Then again, if you use a photo of some stadium filled with thousands of people, the rules are different because it's considered a public event.

4. **Another area to be careful with is taking photos that have recognizable products in them.** You may think you're doing a service to companies like Apple and Nike if you have images with their logos in them. They may think otherwise, and some companies have whole teams of people scouring the Internet for people using their trademarks without permission.

I'm not trying to scare you but instead to sensitize you to this reality when it comes to businesses of any size using images of people and other valuable things. Fortunately, it's possible to be quite creative and still get lots of images. If you own an animal-feed store, then instead of taking a photo of lots of Purina animal-feed bags, you could get a close-up shot of someone's hands holding cracked corn.

Here's the thing about good photography these days: your cell phone likely has a high-quality camera that's better than anything we had 20 years ago. You can take great photos and use the many filters on your phone to ensure that what you post looks great.

How Do I Know If I've Found the Right Person to Do Social Media for Me?

Let's say you have a niece or employee who's amazing at Facebook and you'd like to work out an arrangement where she could do your posts in exchange for something.

Regardless of whether you're dealing with a family member, friend, or even an outside entity, I strongly recommend that you begin the process on a trial basis. In other words, don't say to someone, "I'd like to make you my social-media manager." If it doesn't work out, it's much more difficult to unwind the function if you've said that.

It's much better to ask someone, "Hey, would you be able to take some pictures for me? I'd love to see which ones you think would work well on social media." Then see what you get. If those pictures look good to you, then you can say, "Would you be willing to do a couple of posts for me?" If both of you liked that process, then you can ask the person to do five more, then 10, and so on. If it wasn't so great, then there's no commitment to unwind.

That's even true when it comes to hiring a professional. If this whole area of social media is relatively new to you, you should not be signing some agreement for a comprehensive social-media campaign for substantial money, regardless of how motivated you are. Start small. Hire someone off Upwork.com to do a handful of posts, and take things from there. Down the road you can worry about making an arrangement more permanent.

How Do I Measure Success with Social Media?

First, make sure that you don't take an overly short-term view and expect results immediately. Remember, you are building a relationship with your brand, and that takes time. Your social-media effort is much more like growing a crop and less like pulling a rabbit out of a hat. Quite literally you are trying to grow a following that engages with your posts and looks forward to the next one. In addition, your steady efforts are designed so that the social-media visibility algorithms sit up (as much as computers can sit up), take notice, and think, *Hey, this business is getting steady growth in followers and their engagement. We like that. We're going to start to highlight this business a bit more in our pages, and see if they keep it up. If so, we'll highlight them even more.*

One success measure you should not adopt is how many "likes" you get. The problem is that research has shown that likes do not translate into the actions businesses want their customers to take, such as buying something.[8] Instead, they're just likes.

A better measure is "total engagement." That encompasses everything, including likes, clicks, whether people stop scrolling for even just one second to look at your photo or post, and how long they spend on your content. If you can gradually increase that engagement month after month, then you'll know that you're on the right path and your content efforts are having a positive effect on your social-media sites.

~~~

As powerful as social media can be, you are in the fortunate position of potentially having many other effective tools to grow your business. That's what we cover next.

12

Power Tools

I Am Not referring to those other kinds of power tools. What we will learn about in this chapter are quite a few tools that you can immediately apply in your business to grow it. Some of them are useful in certain circumstances, and others are vital for every small business to have.

A Robust Payment System

There are two kinds of features with products and services: the kind that are highly visible when done well and the kind that are invisible when done well.

The first kind is obvious. If I just had an amazing experience—a great day skiing or boating, say, or a juicy steak with family and friends—I'm probably pretty happy.

On the other hand, we take a lot of things for granted. Most of us never give electricity a thought, until the power goes out. We notice the wings on an airplane, and then forget about them, although we trust them with our lives.

In a sense, the whole system of getting and making payments is like wings on a plane or your electrical outlet. You very much need payments to work, and only really notice when a problem occurs.

I *know* you've been in this situation: you decide on a product and put it in your online shopping cart. You go to check out, fill in all the details including your credit card, and hit send.

Then nothing.

No confirmation, no error message—just nothing. Now what? You just attempted to send a business money, maybe a lot of money. You don't want to click the button again and risk being charged twice.

Does this sound familiar? Can you think of another case where you can go from happy, expectant buyer to infuriated consumer in 30 seconds flat?

Deluxe started in the payments business by inventing the checkbook, and more than a century later we're more involved than ever in both physical and digital payments. In fact, we process $2.8 trillion a year. Yes, I mean trillion. We acquired First American Payments to help small businesses accept credit cards too. This is all to say that we know a thing or two about businesses and their payment systems.

So from a small-business perspective, what do you need to know? Here's what makes a great payment system:

- It needs to allow the business to receive funds in multiple ways. Depending on the types of customers you have, they may want to pay you using cash, check, credit cards, debit cards, GooglePay, ApplePay, Venmo, Zelle, ACH . . . the list can be staggering. More on this in a minute.
- The system also needs to be flexible in terms of how the business sends funds: some vendors want you to pay them through direct deposit, but others will accept or require credit cards, paper checks, international foreign-exchange systems, and so on. Some vendors are very specific about the remittance data (details that must accompany any payment to them).
- Your payment system must interface with your accounting software, in order to save you unbelievable amounts of frustration with documenting transaction details.
- The system must be exceedingly robust in terms of security against hacking, for obvious reasons.

- The payment system must be able to grow as your business grows. You simply can't be swapping out payment systems while you're trying to run a business and provide seamless service to customers.
- Finally, for all this complexity, the system must not cost you an arm and a leg.

Kind of a daunting list, right? There are companies that can help, including First American Payment Systems, a Deluxe company: https://www.first-american.net.

I need to make a point here: there is a reason why Deluxe still sends out 150,000 packages of checks a day, and that is due to how small businesses pay each other. When the produce distributor or fishmonger shows up at the back door of the restaurant to unload the week's food, they likely aren't going to do that until they can leave with a check in hand. The same goes for Maria at the Eclectic Shop in Wabash, Indiana. She can't unload a new shipment of Taproot T-shirts without writing a check. And if you planned any work on your house, chances are the contractor will not take credit cards. Checks remain an essential payment vehicle for businesses.

You're no stranger to lots of detail, given what we've covered in this book. Fortunately, you can follow a process that can identify the right payment system for your business. Here are the steps:

1. **Watch out for anyone who claims that a single payment type can meet all of the needs of a small business.** Each payment type has advantages and drawbacks. If you go with a provider who has oversimplified things, you'll end up paying too much, the customer experience will be poor, or both. There are no magic bullets in the world of payments.
2. **Know your customers.** We gave you the same advice in Chapter 11 about how to choose the best social-media platforms for your customers. The same is true here.

    For example, some businesses, like sandwich shops, have lots of small transactions, while others, like building contractors, have just a few large transactions per month. In addition, the demographics of your customer base is important. Younger customers often prefer systems like Venmo or Zelle, but these don't work at physical stores. ApplePay and GooglePay do work at physical stores but generally require an advanced terminal to accept credit cards too. Being able to accept checks in a physical store can help that store reach clients who don't use credit or debit cards. Some businesses may prefer paper checks.

This gets back to what we discussed way back in Chapter 2 about knowing your numbers. The same transaction can have fees of 30 dollars or 30 cents, depending on the payment system. When you know your customers and transactions, you can work with an advisor to craft a solution that balances cost with convenience.

3. **Speak with someone about the choices.** The payment landscape changes constantly, given how much money is involved. It's a full-time job just to stay on top of the world of payments; you already have a full-time job with your business.

I think our Deluxe advisors are great at this, but you may also find good advice wherever you bank, or from advisors that other small businesses in your area are happy with.

Targeted Promotional Merchandise

Isn't it interesting how some of the most powerful positions in our society wear promotional merchandise?—except they don't call it that. Doctors wear white coats, university grads wear gowns with the school colors and insignia on formal occasions, and the military has all kinds of uniforms.

These different types of garments convey messages of professionalism in different walks of life. What's also interesting is how some businesses use this phenomenon to its full advantage and others do not. We've seen many episodes of *SBR* in which the polo shirts, aprons, and other wear make the owners and staff look like a million bucks. In a sense it's another hallmark of moving from a hobby to a business. It is one of the things that Amanda and our Deluxe team make sure we do for business owners: we engage our promotional solutions segment to create promotional wear for the businesses with their logo and name on it. Notice the look on their faces when they see their new logo with the name of their company on a quality garment: the pride comes through.

Another great aspect of using quality promotional merchandise is how it has the power to make small businesses look like much larger ones. As we discussed earlier about branding, lots of what a business does sends signals. Big businesses can show how big they are with shiny skyscrapers, massive websites, and Super Bowl commercials. But when it comes to polo shirts, shopping bags, business cards, and other gear, the small business can have every bit as high-quality a brand message as the big dogs.

Given that we have a very active promotional merchandise division at Deluxe, we see all sorts of ways that businesses approach their promotional efforts. What you should not adopt as your only tool is the "spray and pray" approach. That's where someone orders many thousands of door hangers, lawn signs, and other materials and kind of carpet-bombs an area. As noted earlier in the book, that can work, but it tends to be a one-shot effort that simply fades away in the next storm. As I said before, business building is a long-term proposition.

Here's the way that we've found works well for small businesses:

First, know your audience. When you know them, it will be clearer what kinds of merchandise they may appreciate. When people on Wall Street close on a big transaction, somebody will distribute beautiful etched-glass "tombstones" that list the transaction details. It's right for that audience.

At Deluxe, we support a luxury automaker that enters their automobiles in a variety of famous races. For this auto manufacturer, we embroider ultra-luxury jackets, caps, golf shirts, and more that they sell to customers at the race events.

We also support neighborhood dry cleaners and jewelry stores that use custom forms that proudly display their logo. The corner pizzeria offers free logo pens and refrigerator magnets.

In the case of Nooma Yoga Studio in Season 4, Episode 5, they had three studios and were eyeing even more expansion, including franchising. As a result, some of their merchandise was high-end water bottles and shopping bags to convey the high-end feeling to customers and potential investors alike.

On the other hand, if you're a pizza parlor, knowing your audience and numbers may mean that your smartest move is to have your brand on magnets in the shape of a delicious pizza for when hungry people raid the refrigerator.

Second, be strategic about where you use promotional material. What parts of the transaction do you want to reinforce the most? In the case of El Mercado Market in Season 4, Episode 4, they wanted customers to think of their market when doing their regular food shopping. Printed shopping bags were a no-brainer as both a service to customers and as little billboard ads scattered across town every day.

Third, test. You want your promotional dollars to work hard for you and make even more dollars. Therefore, keep an eye on when you introduce new merchandise versus sales. Another savvy way to measure results is to use different phone numbers. The cost of additional phone numbers has come way down in recent years. You could have a different phone number on your pizza magnets; when people call that number, a system like CallRail.com can log the call and redirect the caller seamlessly to your main number. Then you can look at a report to see how many people used the pizza-magnet number last month.

The beauty of promotional merchandise is that you can crawl, then walk, then run with it as your business grows. Modern manufacturing techniques mean you don't have to buy 5,000 units of something to see if it will have a positive effect on your business.

A great success story came from Season 5, Episode 6 with Vineyards Golf Course in Fredonia, New York. During the pandemic, golf was one of the few activities that was allowed throughout the country—even during lockdowns. Golf boomed in 2020, given how it was an outside activity and physical distancing was relatively easy. Vineyards rode that wave, yet they had lacked the swag that other golf courses had. We helped them out, providing shirts, sweatshirts, golf balls, and other items with the Vineyards logo. Owner Debbie Mancuso said that they sold out quickly with the new logo; it became a new revenue stream that helped them thrive during the pandemic. Having customers wearing Vineyards logo gear around town was great advertising and a simultaneous endorsement from the wearer.

Tools for Competitive Intelligence

I hope that I've sufficiently hammered home in previous chapters the idea that you need to stay on top of what your competitors are up to. It is not because you want to follow them, but because your potential customers are continuously trying to weigh the offerings of different businesses as the solution to their current problem. If you can help them do that, you'll stand apart from the crowd.

But short of going undercover into your competitors' businesses, how can you keep tabs on them? Stated another way, how might a smart competitor keep tabs on you?

The most straightforward and logical way to keep tabs on them is to visit their websites regularly. See what they're up to; take notes on interesting products, services, or features of their website. You don't need to copy them exactly, but you might get inspiration about something you could change in your business.

A great tool for saving time while keeping tabs on your competition is FollowThatPage.com. It is free and will tell you any time a page has changed. For example, if you want to know whether a competitor changes its prices, you can take the web address or URL of that pricing page and put it into FollowThatPage.com. Then you give that service your email address and tell it how often to check the competitor's site. It will monitor the site for any changes whatsoever and will alert you if it found one. It's excellent.

Another related tool is Google Alerts.[1] This tool does not monitor one specific page but instead looks across the web and tells you when it finds new instances of a phrase. For example, you can tell it to monitor your name or the name of your business, and it will alert you if a web page is published with that name. You might create free Google Alerts using your competitors' names or certain product names. That way you can easily stay on top of press releases and new pages on a website about them. You would still need FollowThatPage if you wanted to know about the slightest changes to a particular page.

Another good tool for competitor intelligence is spyfu.com. It is a massive database of ads and other details from businesses around the globe. You can type in a competitor's website and see exactly what paid-search ads that competitor has run over time. If you see lots of changes every month, that might mean that the competitor is testing different approaches. But if you then see that one ad has stuck around for a long time, it may mean that it's working well.

If you do find an ad like that, you should not copy it exactly, but instead can run an ad on a similar theme, and see what happens.

All of this competitive information I've mentioned is available publicly on the Internet, so it's not spying in the sense of breaking into anything. Using it is just being a well-informed business owner about the useful information that exists for the taking.

Tools for Intelligence on Your Own Site

The first tool you need is Google Analytics. I have mentioned Google a lot in this book. The simple truth is that Google has become ubiquitous. Its size and dominance of the search space make it impossible to ignore. Google also has significant tools for small-business owners to use in order to be competitive. Google Analytics is a free service that can give you an astonishing amount of detail about your website visitors and what they do. You'll probably need someone to help you to install a small bit of information from Google on your website. Then you'll be able to answer questions like:

- How many people visited my site today/this week/this month/in the past three years, whenever?
- Where do I get most of my visitors? Do they come from social media, or from my paid search, or elsewhere?
- Of all the sales I've made online in the past five months, how many came from social media versus organic search versus paid search?
- Which are my most popular pages, so I can write more about those themes?
- What percent of my visitors come to my site once, never to return, versus have returned once, twice, or even 10 times?
- And about a hundred other questions.

It's an important use of your time to review Google Analytics perhaps monthly, gain insights from it, and make the necessary course corrections.

Grown-Up Moment

Most business owners do nothing with Google Analytics. I suspect many don't know about it, but for those who do, it feels like work to gain these insights, and they'd be correct. But you've done all the obvious stuff to grow your business and it's not been sufficient, right? Having the insights on visitors that Google Analytics provides for free can help you make smarter choices about what to do more of, and what to stop doing.

The next tool you need is Google Search Console. Again, you should probably ask someone to help you install this service on your site. If you went to Fiverr.com, you would see people offering to do it for literally five dollars. The tool is free.

Google Search Console basically shows you the health of your site, in terms of whether any pages are broken or have other problems. It will also tell you which pages it knows about. You may find out that Google has not scanned one of your pages, and that's why you've been scratching your head and wondering why you're seeing no signups or sales from the page.

When you do create a new page, you can go to Search Console and tell Google about it, so it will be indexed or reviewed as soon as possible.

Yet another reason to get it is that Search Console has a Mobile Usability Report that will tell you if certain elements of your site are broken when viewed on mobile devices.

This One Will Blow You Away

What few people realize is how much of our online behavior is recorded. The way I see it, why not have the benefit of that information if it's already available, done ethically, and it's for the ultimate benefit of customers?

There is a category of tools that allow you to see exactly what each individual visitor does on your website. And I mean exactly. Here's what they allow you to do:

- You can see a recording of each visitor's mouse on your homepage, as she or he moves it around.
- You see where the mouse moves, and where it stops.
- It shows you how far down the page someone scrolls.
- If someone seems really engaged, you can see the person scroll back up to the top of the page and click different menu items.
- You'll have this for every page the person visits, what time of day it was, how long the person was on your site, and if the person took any action on your site like filling out a form or playing a video.

The first reaction when you see this might be: *Wow, that's kinda creepy. I feel like I'm spying on people.* But the thing is, you can only do this for your own site; you can't see what people do elsewhere.

Pretty soon you may realize how invaluable this tool is to understanding your visitors and customers. For example: Why is this person clicking and clicking on something that is not a link? What's going on? Well maybe you underlined it for emphasis, but people are accustomed to thinking that underlining means something's a link. Maybe what you should do is create a link there, to give people additional information. This is common with images on sites. If you see people clicking on images, and nothing happens when they do, then make something happen.

The opposite is also true. Let's say you have a link somewhere and you really want people to click it, because it's about your Fall Clearance Event. When you watch the visitor recordings, they seem to blow right past that link and scroll down the page. What's going on there?

What you may discover is that their eyes are drawn to an image of an attractive person, or an ice cream sundae, or a dog—all of which are more interesting than a link.

This is important: some research suggests that there is a connection between where people move their mouse and where their eyes are focused. You'll even see it as people will be reading a paragraph on your site, and their mouse cursor is going back and forth.

In the earlier case, you have a theory that visitors may be ignoring your link in favor of the dog. So, you can try taking the dog off the page, or moving it elsewhere, and see if you get more clicks on the link.

Another great use of this tool is on your shopping cart or checkout pages. You may find that people fill out a form halfway and then suddenly just stop and leave. Bunches of people may be doing that.

With this sort of tool, you can study the behavior and realize, for instance, that they're leaving at the point where you ask them for their cell number. *Hmmm, I wonder if my visitors are thinking that I might spam their cell phone, text them at all hours, or even sell their cell number to someone?*

With that idea, you can test some solutions. You can explain what you're going to do with the cell number; or you can make it optional. You might just take it off entirely if you don't truly need it, and see if that reduces shopping-cart abandonment.

This is sophisticated stuff you're doing! You are intensively focusing on your visitors and customers, so that you can make adjustments and improve their experience with you. That's a win/win.

I really like a tool in this category called Mouseflow.com. It has a free account where you can see all of the above for a certain number of visitors per month. If you have more traffic than that, and want to get insights on all the visitors, then their paid services are relatively inexpensive.

Low-Cost Insights

Let's say you are really torn between two variations of a new logo, and you just can't decide. Or it might be a question about two different images on your site, or two headlines.

You can go with your gut, but wouldn't it be nice to get some quick feedback from people who are similar to your customers? You can do it with a tool called Pickfu.com. It is a service where, for a few bucks, you can choose from among about 45 characteristics. These are things like dog owners, gamers, married, male, and so on.

Then you upload two variations of the thing you want feedback on. They'll then have 50 or more people view your two versions, choose one, and do a written explanation of why they like it. This is an excellent way of taking some of the guesswork out of deciding what might resonate best with your target audience.

Using Video Effectively

Video on your site and in your social-media posts can be a very powerful power tool indeed. Words are amazing for getting complicated concepts across, and video delivers a different message into the brains of customers. You need both.

Earlier I described how people can pay too much for their websites because it all seems too complicated. The same can sometimes be true with video. You can produce surprisingly good videos on a small budget.

If you look at Flow Studios, the video professionals we use for the *SBR* series—wow. They're amazing. But as a small-business owner, be careful to not get depressed and think: *I could never do video. Just look at that Deluxe show—it takes a whole team of professionals.*

It's true that Flow Studios has a large staff of professionals for a network TV production, but it's also true that most of the video people see on YouTube, Facebook, and elsewhere is nowhere near as professional as the *SBR* production. It doesn't need to be. Visitors to business websites are looking for authenticity instead of hype, as we talked about in Chapter 7 on persuasion.

I thought it would be helpful to cover some key questions about using video in your business.

What equipment do I need to get started with videos? If we're talking about simply getting started, you can use a recent smartphone. Plenty of videos are shot that way. The key is to get started, and not to feel like you need to collect a lot of gear before you could ever shoot videos. Getting going *now* with what you have is infinitely preferable to getting around to the perfect setup someday.

Our company knows a guy who is a well-established marketer and has made a lot of money online. He created his dream video-production studio in San Diego, with cameras, computers, lights, and all the extras. It was a six-figure expense.

These days he shoots using his iPhone. Occasionally he'll fire up the fancy studio, but he's found that the immediacy of shooting a short video when he has a good idea is much better than getting his whole crew in. Plus he says his audience is just fine with the simple videos.

For what it's worth, I send video communications to 6,000-plus employees shot on my mobile phone . . . by me. The important point is to communicate authentically. Yes, glossy, well-produced content is fantastic. But getting the message out is more important than gloss.

None of this is to say that you should never have the option of better equipment.

When you do have a few bucks to devote to video, you'll need a video camera; a good, solid tripod; an external microphone (because camera mics are inferior); and some lights to fill in shadows.

Again, look at what Nooma does. Casey Cox and her team are exceptional. Their videos have a professional quality and they use video extremely effectively, showing the movements of a class or the fun their patrons are having on any given day. And they do it with their phones, without a professional videographer on hand.

There's a good video-related company you should follow, called Wistia.com. They have lots of informative videos and blog posts about loads of video topics. They also have a practical gear-buying guide at: https://wistia.com/learn/production/video-gear-guide.

What if I mess up during a video I'm filming? Do I have to start over? No. Let's say you were in the middle of describing something and you briefly lost your train of thought. You can stop filming at that point, remember what you wanted to say, turn it back on and then pick up the description where you left off.

Then it's easy to edit out the moment when you forgot. You can also use video-editing tools to add a little music in the background and many other features. If you use an Apple computer, then iMovie will work just fine, and it's free. If you're on a PC, then Adobe Premiere costs a few dollars a month.

When is it appropriate to use something like Facebook Live versus shooting a video and then editing and uploading it? In case you don't know, services like Facebook Live allow you to do just that: upload your live video directly into Facebook for others to watch in real time.

This can be fun for festivals, speeches, concerts, contests announcements, and other highly visual events. But you definitely need a second videographer to capture the moment properly for later editing. Live video is raw video, and the excitement of the moment can make up for poor video technique. If you want that footage to be engaging later, you'll need the edited version.

What is a good length for my videos? In general, shorter is better. It will allow your video to be suitable for more platforms; besides, if the video is short, you can be more confident that your audience receives the full message and doesn't quit partway through.

Staying under two minutes is a good guideline. In my communications, I force myself to stay under two minutes and try for under 60 seconds. If you can make your point clearly in a short window, your customers will easily "get it." If it takes longer, chances are you're not clear or the product benefit is too hard to understand. When you're working on your talking points remember TV news organizations cover even the most complicated stories in well under two minutes. Don't fall into the self-flattery trap that could make you believe everyone wants to hear all the details of your company or product. They don't, so cut to the chase.

The exception is if you do how-to videos. Those can be significantly longer, because you don't want to miss any steps. Even so, it's a good idea to keep people's attention by hitting the high points and being succinct. You can always refer people to written resources on your website if they need more detail.

What is video hosting, and do I need it? Video is notorious for taking a lot of space to store. If your video is successful and lots of people watch it, the computers storing the video can crash if they're not specifically designed to handle video. So yes, you need video hosting. In other words, whatever hosting you have for your website is unlikely to be adequate if you like to shoot video. In effect you need to rent a firehose that can deliver loads of data instantly, and most web-hosting plans are more like garden hoses, which are fine for text on web pages.

The three big video-hosting platforms are YouTube, Wistia, and Vimeo. If you're just getting started and money is tight, then YouTube is a great choice. In that case, you'd open a free account with YouTube, upload your video there, and they'll give you a link. Then you put that link on your website and the video will play from YouTube when visitors click that link.

The downside to consider with YouTube is that they insert advertisements in your video, or even an outside chance a competitor's ad could appear. You will also see unrelated videos displayed at the end of your video. If you want complete control of how your videos look, then go with an outfit like Wistia.

Where can I get good ideas for videos I might make? One good source for ideas is a service called AnswerThePublic.com. The website is a little weird but the content is great. You can type in a term like "hot yoga" and it will give you a ton of ideas, based on what people have typed into Google. For example, it will list questions like: "What is hot yoga good for?" and "Will hot yoga give me kidney stones?" You can look through dozens of questions and quickly come up with some ideas for videos. For that matter, these could be good topics for web pages, an FAQ, or emails to your list of customers.

~~~

The tools to ensure your business runs smoothly are essential. There is no debating that. What can set your business apart is your people. In the next chapter, we look at how to find the right people and what it will take to keep them to take your business to another level.

13

Your Team

Great vision without great people is irrelevant.

—*Jim Collins*

EVERY BUSINESS STARTS with a dream or a vision. Some of those businesses become big businesses someday. Even large businesses need leadership and vision to succeed. And as you know personally, a great deal can be accomplished by just one person— the owner or the leader— working day and night. But, that's just not enough to truly succeed if a business aspires to be more than a one-person band.

In Chapter 2 we talked about the necessity for brutal honesty and for knowing your "why" when you went from an idea or hobby and became a business, and why you choose to stay in business. For most businesses, there comes a point when the owner must be able to draw a salary from the business, or else the whole effort will crumble from lack of profitability. Then you can get a job working for another business owner who has a better idea, a clearer vision, and the ability to pay you for your services.

The same is true when it comes to the business owner's willingness to work. You may have the most selfless, dedicated approach to work that's possible, but there comes a point when you can't do any more. In fact, you probably can't even sustain the time and effort you're already putting into the business as it is, never mind find a way to grow it.

I'm going to assume that you are willing to delegate—to give capable people clear expectations and the latitude to deliver the needed result. It's easy to say "yes" to yourself here. But, delegation requires trust and acceptance that the task may be done well, even if not exactly how you would have done it.

You may be unwilling to delegate today because you haven't found people you trust. You may be stuck on three common issues: how to find great talent, how to pay for them, and how to manage them. That's what we now cover.

I don't know if you've ever hired and managed people before. I can tell you that it can be the worst of times and the absolute best of times. When it doesn't work out, then it's continuous frustration and friction. You need certain things done and no matter how hard you try, your employee isn't getting the message—or delivers late or sloppily, or in a way that does not appeal to your customers. It's like you thought you were hiring Superman and Dr. Jekyll showed up to work.

The Question Before the Question

You may ask the question "How can I find great talent?" I've discovered that the best answer to that question is actually another question: "How can I make my business a place where great talent wants to work?" We could spend another book on this topic, but we will dive in just a bit here.

This is yet another occasion where you as a business owner need to be brutally honest with yourself. It may be true that you have the passion for this work down to your bones. But what can you offer people with really great talent, such that they too are attracted to your vision?

This is where the various drivers of job satisfaction come in. People are motivated by lots of things:

- Money
- Equity (the promise of money or ownership down the line)
- Fame, or being close to famous people

- A sense of belonging—being part of something bigger than themselves
- Being part of a team
- Cool benefits, employee discounts
- A worthy cause and common goals
- The ability to learn from someone with deep knowledge
- A great working environment
- A short commute
- The realistic promise of great things to come
- Wide latitude or flexibility so the job fits in amazingly well with the rest of the person's life

Maybe you can think of other motivations as well. How many of them can you put on the table right now, realistically?

It's easy to focus on money and think, *I can't pay much, so I guess I'm screwed when it comes to attracting great talent.*

That's a bit of a cop-out. We've all heard the stories of big companies starting as an idea in someone's garage, with people working hard for peanuts at the time. This is not just a high-tech phenomenon: Ray Kroc, the McDonald's founder, hired June Martino to help him with bookkeeping. He couldn't pay her fully in cash, so he gave her stock. She ended up becoming a director of McDonald's.[1]

You may also think, *I'm not trying to build the next McDonald's or Apple, so I don't need to attract super talent, nor can I afford it.*

Take some advice from me, as a former small-business owner and now in my position of running a company with more than 6,000 employees: the quality of your people is the *most effective lever* you have to affect your *success. You MUST attract great talent, as your company can never be better than your weakest employee.*

Jim Collins in *Good to Great* calls this getting the right people on the bus.

I'm very fortunate that Deluxe had an amazing group of dedicated people calling themselves Deluxers even before I was on the scene. In fact, it's one of the main reasons I took the job. But, we've also kept adding new, great talent to help us push ahead even faster.

One of the highest and best uses of your time as a business owner is to think about the list of motivations just mentioned, which ones you can deliver on, and how you can piece together a package of them that will attract great people.

Notice how many of the motivators are potentially within your control, even if you're short on cash. You can create an amazing environment and might be able to mentor people. You may come across some extraordinarily gifted people who have disabilities or health issues, where they don't fit into the standard, Monday-through-Friday, 9-to-5 commuting lifestyle. If you get creative about what you can offer to great people, you could be rewarded, big time.

Your Hiring Process

Is your hiring process helping or hurting your chances of attracting great talent? Let's find out.

- Does your job posting read like some bureaucrat with jargon running through his veins wrote it? Or do you try to sell the position by making the job sound appealing? Would you apply for that job if you were looking for that kind of job?
- When candidates show up for an interview, do you keep them waiting, or seem disinterested in the process? Or do you treat candidates the way you would treat a valued customer? Is your enthusiasm contagious?
- Does it take forever for jobs to be filled, partly due to having no clear criteria for what you're looking for? Even after interviews, do you string people along because you can't make up your mind? Do you respectfully let candidates know you've selected someone else—or wait for them to find out on their own? With every interaction you're building your employment brand, too. Do you want to be known for blowing people off, or respectfully declining? What do you want the unsuccessful candidate to be saying about you to a future recruit?

The most talented people usually have choices. The reality is that if you succeed in having some of them apply for your job, they're checking you out as much as you're checking them out. It's worth your time to make this process be something that impresses your applicants.

Again, it does not cost anything except some thoughtful planning and organizing on your part.

The typical interview process does not shed much light on whether the applicant will be able to do the job. It often starts with questions like: "So tell me about yourself." A half-notch up from that is the question you should already know the answer to, if you have the applicant's resume: "So, what did you do at your last job?"

Traits We Look for in New Hires

As you can imagine, we hire a lot of people at Deluxe, and one of the larger units we have are the call centers. As odd as it may sound, it's not necessarily a plus for people to have worked in a call center before. That's because we find that we need to undo some things they may have learned elsewhere. For example, they may have worked in a highly scripted environment, or where they must sell a certain amount of products each month. That's just not the Deluxe way. Here are five things we look for when hiring; maybe you can benefit from seeking people with these same characteristics.

1. **Leadership and aspiration.** Has this candidate differentiated themselves at school, work, sporting team, club, church, community, or anywhere and been responsible for delivering something of value? Can they explain that accomplishment enthusiastically and with pride? These people are capable of getting others to positively engage on a challenge. Mark Sanborn has written two books on the importance of leadership, initiative, and aspiration, *The Fred Factor* and *You Don't Need a Title to Be a Leader*.[2] Both books talk about the difference one individual can make if they choose to act and lead. I try to fill my teams with "Freds" and people who will lead no matter what.

2. **Curiosity and creativity.** Does the candidate like to learn and make a difference? The most creative people make every day unique. They listen and come up with interesting solutions to customers' or the business's issues.

3. **Grit.** Does the candidate have a good work ethic and is able to push through a tough situation to get the job done? Do they have

what your mother called good old-fashioned "stick-to-it-iveness"? Or is this person a "snowflake" who will melt in the slightest sunshine or first little bump in the road? Angela Duckworth has written an impressive and important book on this topic, titled *Grit*.[3] I recommend it.

4. **Retail experience or exposure to small business.** The candidate might have worked for a Starbucks or Macy's at some point, or some other place where they developed skills at interacting with people. We are a team culture at Deluxe. People who have had to work with other people to get things done are essential to our model. Similarly, it's great when someone has direct experience with running a small business. We've also found that it's a big plus to find people whose family has been involved in small businesses. These people can truly relate to small businesses that are Deluxe customers: "Hey, I watched my parents get up every morning at 4 to open their bakery," or whatever the case may be. No doubt the whole family had some type of duties in the small business, and that's a real asset.

5. **Character and teamwork.** In his book *Give and Take*, Adam Grant writes about the notion of "givers," who make the best employees.[4] I think the book is an excellent guide about team selection and effectiveness. Grant provides many great questions designed to find givers.

As the CEO I try to ask Grant's questions to help me find people who fit the mold of being a giver. I want to know not so much the dates and roles that are already on the resume, but the character of the person behind the resume—the "how" and "why" they got things done. To get insights into that, I always ask every candidate this question: "I want to know the three times when you have failed, where you missed quota, underdelivered, or where you disappointed yourself. More importantly, I'm interested in how you put those lessons to work to do better." I explain to the candidate that I'm not really focused much on what they failed at, just why. What I really want to know is what the candidate learned from the failure or disappointment, and how they are now a different and better person and employee as a result. Did they productively engage others to help along the way? Did they own the outcome? Did they help others (being a giver) to help them succeed?

I'll hear such interesting responses, which tell so much so quickly about a candidate. Some people will describe how they made a big mistake one time, or how they got fired. They'll talk about how they picked themselves up and went on, and how their future approach to similar situations changed. This sort of answer is what impresses me. The candidates have the self-awareness that bad things happen to everyone, and if you haven't experienced a failure or disappointment you probably haven't ever tried at anything very hard. It's all about what you do to recover and grow from mistakes that counts.

It is a very bad sign if the candidate doesn't have any failures, disappointments, lessons to share, or examples of how they helped others. I won't hire anyone who explains their own failures as the result of someone else's actions. That person will never be successful at our company because they don't hold themselves responsible for the outcome of their work, and they clearly don't fit Grant's model of being a giver.

From time to time I'll hear nonresponse responses where the person is showing their character, and it's not good. It usually goes like this: "I've had situations where perhaps I was not quite able to meet expectations, but here's the thing about me: my hallmark is I always succeed. I always get it right."

Uh huh. Next.

Everyone has failures and makes mistakes, and Asian cultures have made a particular point to capture multiple stories and allegories to share wisdom from failures and more. The Zen master Shunryu Suzuki tells the following story:

> It is said that there are four kinds of horses: excellent ones, good ones, poor ones, and bad ones. The best horse will run slow and fast, right and left, at the driver's will, before it sees the shadow of the whip. The second-best will run as well as the first one does, just before the whip reaches its skin. The third one will run when it feels pain on its body. The fourth will run after the pain penetrates to the marrow of its bones. You can imagine how difficult it is for the fourth one to learn how to run!

When we hear this story, almost all of us want to be the best horse. If it is impossible to be the best one, we want to be second best. . . . When you are determined to practice [Zen], you will find the worst horse is the most valuable one. In your very imperfections you will find the basis of your firm, way-seeking mind.[5]

I've lost count of the number of times I've messed up, and of course I wish it were fewer. But I believe I've learned from and applied those lessons to make me better. I've found my best team members have struck out plenty themselves too. What they do before the next at-bat tells me a lot about who they are.

Finally, I pay lots of attention to building a cohesive team. I once had a boss who was famous for saying: "how they 'fit' in the locker room is as important to how well they play on the field." He called this the "locker room test." A great player who is a prima donna who is only interested in themselves can destroy a team, and is clearly not a giver. A very good player who can rally the team is far better than a great player who can't be a team player.

References

I want to pass along one more suggestion about how to size up candidates. Let's say you've interviewed several people for a position, and you've narrowed things down to a couple of people. Both have good resumes, and both impressed you during their interview. Now it's time to check references.

We all know that people will put down the best references they can, and also that when you call a reference, he or she is unlikely to be very negative. How then can you make the most of the reference check?

Here's what I do. I talk with the reference for a little while at the beginning in a friendly and conversational manner, to kind of warm up the conversation. Then I ask the normal sort of questions, like how the person was as a team member, work ethic, character, and so on. Then I like to ask the following:

Let's just say for a moment that I hired this person and let's just say hypothetically that you and I were having another conversation a year from now. At that time, I told you I had to let the person go.

In this hypothetical situation, what would come to your mind as the likely reasons why I had to let the person go?

Then you shut up and listen. What you hear will tell you plenty.

Alternatives to Hiring

In this book I've mentioned several times that you can find some excellent talent at places like Upwork and Fiverr, and that's true. In fact, some of the best talent there are people who have that need for very flexible work hours. That's why they're so good but not working full-time at a regular job. Other people have quit the corporate world or have advanced degrees and now are trying to build a resume with some work history and potential references. Six months from now they'll be fully booked, but at the moment these very talented people are available to help you.

Of course, some jobs require people to be physically present at the store or office. But if that is not the case with the job you need filled, it's a great idea to look for talent on these platforms, for several other reasons as well.

- You can read reviews from other customers who have hired them.
- Often they will have uploaded a portfolio of work samples, so you can get an even better idea of their skills compared to what you need.
- You can hire people to do a small task, so you risk very little. You explain that if that task works out well, there's a lot more where that came from.
- This toe-in-the-water approach works for both parties to see if the chemistry is right.
- This sort of low-risk hiring may help to refine your ideas around the sort of job description and person you need for a permanent position.

~~~

Few things are as important as hiring, as we discussed. Yet owners never have the luxury of focusing on one aspect of their business for long; too many things need continuous attention, even when things are going well. The next chapter—the last chapter—is about some ways to make that work.

14

Eyes Wide Open

FOR THOUSANDS OF years, people have pursued the dream of someday stumbling on a way to turn lead into gold. As a small-business owner, you've already done it.

You had this crazy idea for a business, and you couldn't get it out of your mind. You took materials that were available to anyone, but you put them together in a way that created enough value for customers to pay you to deliver your product or service. You are indeed an alchemist.

People who have never taken the leap to become small-business owners do not know how difficult it can be, even when things are going well. Like the performer who spins many plates on top of sticks, even when it's all working well, it requires your complete attention, or else things can come crashing down in an instant. Quite literally all can be lost in a minute.

In these pages we've talked a lot about how to keep all those plates spinning, and how to grow your paying audience. For this last chapter, I'd like to give you six more suggestions for making progress despite whatever challenges you face.

Small Hinges Swing Big Doors

Sometimes the difference between where you are now and where you want to be can be through smaller adjustments than you might think. We've seen in several *SBR* episodes how a minor price increase had the potential to keep an entire business from closing.

Although pricing is just one of the hinges in your business, it's worth your time to review your pricing regularly, and to get creative with it.

In his very good book *Influence*, Robert Ciandini talks about how a woman who owned a small jewelry store was having real trouble selling some turquoise jewelry. She tried various sales techniques but nothing seemed to work.

Finally she threw up her hands and before leaving town on business, she scrawled a note to her assistant: "Everything in this display case, price x ½."

When she returned from her trip the owner was relieved but not surprised that cutting the price worked, because the jewelry had all sold.

But the assistant had misread the note and had doubled the price, causing the jewelry to sell out.[1]

Another aspect of your business has a hinge worth scrutinizing. In Season 2, Episode 4, we saw the pressures that Robert and Alison Angelaccio were under to run Annabella's Italian Restaurant. One of the counterintuitive, less-is-more changes the Deluxe team suggested was to shorten the menu to make the restaurant more successful. While not a previously obvious answer, Robert and Alison were open to the idea, and it was a positive move.

What is hanging around your neck that would be a big relief to have dealt with? Devote some time to identifying all that you can. Once you see them, they may be like objects in your sideview mirror: the solution may be closer than you think.

When Circumstances Change, Take Time to Think

Another excellent book I can recommend to you is *The Road Less Stupid*, by serial entrepreneur Keith Cunningham.[2] After 40 years of starting and running businesses, his secret weapon for success is to carve out 30 to 45 minutes of uninterrupted thinking time on a regular basis. He has a whole structure for determining how to use that time to maximum advantage.

I am proud to say that when COVID hit, Deluxe got together and thought creatively about what the business needed to do—immediately—to support our customers. We hit the phones and talked with customers about what they needed the most. We found these businesses needed what the whole world was in short supply of at the time: PPE (personal protective equipment).

We knew nothing about PPE when the crisis hit. No market insight. No source of supply. No sales materials. No way to sell the products or even take an order. No way to bill a customer. But the team did some hard—and fast—thinking and realized that what we were good at was working with suppliers around the world, and getting high-quality materials to customers in a hurry.

We were not alone in this equivalent of a war effort. Other businesses retooled and figured out how they could manufacture face masks or whatever. But I'm incredibly proud of our team. They were just as concerned as anyone else for their families and themselves—but they delivered more than $25 million worth of masks, gloves, sanitizer, thermometers, and other PPE gear in just 90 days.

Even if sometimes we're not facing a pandemic, you need to carve out that time to think about what's changed in your competitive environment. No one else will do this important work for you.

Count Yourself In

I've talked about this before, but I simply must emphasize its importance: you need to take care of yourself, or else this whole small-business experiment will fall to pieces.

You put yourself last; that's your style. You also feel like you can always work a little harder, for a little longer; that's also your style. But you've used up all your "somedays," as in "someday I'll pay myself." This book is a failure if I do not convince you to sit down and build a plan for exactly when you will pay yourself a decent income. Now is the time to ask your "why" and start to plan your "how."

Execute on the Fundamentals, Even When They Are Tiresome to You

Deluxe is headquartered in Minnesota. Our friends to the east—in Wisconsin—had a legendary football coach by the name of Vince Lombardi. Coach Lombardi was famous for starting training camp for the Green Bay Packers by saying, "Gentlemen, this is a football."[3]

He knew that games and championships were won by executing on the boring fundamentals, which are called fundamentals for a reason: they form the basis of success.

It may be useful to think about being an instrument player or the grand marshal of a parade. You have a three-mile route and you're going to play your songs several dozen times. By about Mile 1 you are utterly sick of hearing those songs; yet to the bystanders lining the parade route, your tunes are fresh. The parade is for their benefit.

As tired as you are with reviewing financials, surveying customers, reviewing your marketing methods, and telling your story to prospects, those are your marching orders for now. You are tired of your story but today's audience has not yet heard about you. Therefore, execute on your primary tasks despite your urge to do something fresh. Move that football down the field for the thousandth time, despite your urge to quit.

Don't Suffer in Silence

The only thing new under the sun is the history you don't know. With the exception of some cutting-edge technology, most business practices and challenges have been around for a long time.

I said before that no matter what success you've had in business, there's always someone ahead of you and behind you. Someone out there has the solution to your current challenges; you just need to connect with that person.

Your first step is to articulate what you need as clearly as possible. This is the time to get specific, as we discussed in Chapter 4. Instead of saying "My business is treading water," it's more productive to say "I don't know how to do fundraising and now that's become something

I must do on top of my other duties." The more specific you get about the gap you see, the more likely you will find someone online, at the Chamber of Commerce, or in the business association who's been there and goes, "Oh yeah, I was there two years ago. Here's what I did. . . ."

You can ask for help not only from other small-business owners, but also from your customers. We saw this happen big-time during the COVID crisis, where people knew restaurants were hurting badly so customers made a point of getting takeout meals and cocktails.[3] We are in this together: even fierce Olympic competitors have been known to help each other across the finish line.[4]

Beware of Shiny Objects

A million brass bands are out there, trying to distract you with the loud promise of their revolutionary approach. They'll proclaim that "Google is dead" or "Everything you know about business is wrong" as a way of hyping their latest gimmicky solution.

Certainly in our lifetime we've seen revolutionary changes, like the Internet and cloud. But the truly remarkable changes need no carnival barker to yell at us about how great they are.

Business success is a matter of staying focused on the great constants of knowing your numbers, staying close to your customers through continual dialogue, delivering more than they expect, caring for and building up your team, and other unchanging business skills. Dabblers and hobbyists consider it boring; I call it "minding the store."

~~~

What an honorable calling you've undertaken. You have risked years of your life and all of your savings to create something that's larger than any one person. You provide services to your community and create jobs. Occasionally it feels like your reward is sacrificed nights, weekends, and even years, in order to keep it all moving forward.

A wise person once said: "A ship in harbor is safe, but that is not what ships are built for."[6] You have built your ship and assembled a crew for it. You've set sail and quickly learned how some very strong forces can toss you about. You will not steer a straight path toward your destination, because you must make numerous course corrections just to stay afloat.

That's okay. With your eyes open to dangers and also to guidance from stars and lighthouses, you can make this journey. I can't wait to hear about the stories you'll be able to tell.

Now go for it!

Epilogue: When to Abandon the Dream?

THE SAD TRUTH: According to the latest information on the small business failure rate published by the U.S. Bureau of Labor Statistics:

- **Roughly 20%** of small businesses fail within the *first year*.
  21.6% of small businesses founded in March 2017 were closed by March 2018.
- **Roughly 33%** *of small businesses fail within two years*.
  31% of small businesses founded in March 2016 were closed by March 2018.
- **Roughly 50%** of small businesses fail within *five years*.
  49.3% of small businesses founded in March 2013 were closed by March 2018.
- **Roughly 66%** of small businesses fail within *10 years*.
  66.3% of small businesses founded in March 2008 were closed by March 2018.[1]

Businesses fail for many reasons. For starters, it is a competitive market. Virtually none of the failures come from an owner who doesn't care or who hasn't tried hard or passionately pursued their dream.

America has democratic political and capitalist economic systems. I'm not here to debate the merits of political or economic systems; I'm simply stating the current reality of today.

In our system, everyone gets to vote for their leaders at the ballot box. And everyone gets to vote with their dollars and buy the products and services of their choosing. Government doesn't mandate what you can or cannot buy or from whom (mostly), or what goods or services you should or shouldn't want. We have the luxury of living in a free country with a free market. That structure gives us the opportunity to start a business.

The good news for all of us as consumers: through this system we can expect ever-improving products and a rising standard of living from the pressure competition creates. Business, especially small business, is at the very heart of this economic competition that benefits everyone ultimately, even if not equally.

A new business can start at any time to challenge any other business. This is good, as it ensures that the consumer will ultimately have choices to get the best product or service for the best price.

If you're a business owner, that means you must compete. In every competition, there are successes and failures, winners and losers. So, as the sobering data at the beginning of this chapter shows, businesses may be successful for a time, but most eventually fail.

There is no shame in failing, and I think there is intense pride in trying. Someone will find the right formula, and it might as well be you.

Common Causes of Business Failure

Philip Kotler, the famous Northwestern University Kellogg Graduate School of Management professor, and father of modern marketing, created the four Ps of marketing and business success, and recently added a fifth. The five are: product, pricing, placement, promotion, and purpose. If a business misses on any of these five, the chance of success falls significantly.

With these five Ps in mind, here are a few examples of how businesses fail:

■ **Product.** Sometimes a business fails because the product or business was not competitive in the market. The neighborhood has too many businesses like it, and the competitors just have a better product or service. Frequently, I've seen business owners enamored with their product, because it appeals to them personally. However, sometimes that appeal is very limited, with few others interested. This is different than not having a competitive product. In this case the market doesn't want the product even though the business owner wishes otherwise. Products or businesses in markets without profitable demand might be better suited to be a hobby than a business.

■ **Price.** Sometimes a business fails because the price was wrong— the product cost too much to make relative to what the customer is willing to pay. Chevys and Bentleys are both cars that do exactly the same thing, transporting you from Point A to Point B. One costs tens of thousands of dollars to buy and make. The other costs hundreds of thousands to buy and make. A Bentley costs far more to make than a Chevy, but there are consumers willing to pay for the Bentley. But many more customers have the resources for a Chevy. Sometimes a business tries to pass a Chevy off as a Bentley, or very commonly, businesses have built a Bentley, but the market is only interested in transportation at the Chevy price. In *SBR* we've also seen businesses not charging enough for their products or services. The business owner was concerned about charging friends and neighbors more. Rather than raising prices to a fair level, the business risked failure.

■ **Placement.** Sometimes a business fails because market demand in your area and distribution locations are not enough for the product being offered. Perhaps the product would sell well in a suburban Whole Foods, but you can only get placement in rural Dollar General. The product might be excellent, but the market area or places of distribution don't work. The business might have worked in an area with different demographics or being sold through different channels of distribution.

■ **Promotion.** The business couldn't reach its target audience with its message about the product at a low enough cost, or effectively. As a result the business was not profitable and failed.

■ **Purpose.** In Chapter 2 we talked about "why." Why are you starting or running your business? This is the same as "purpose," or why the business exists. Of course, every business exists to support the owner and workers. Sometimes businesses fail because the purpose, or the "why," is no longer relevant. Sometimes, the "why" isn't strong enough for the owners to continue to invest their time and effort. Sometimes, the community or market simply moves past the company's purpose. Businesses fail when their purpose and their "why" no longer make sense or deliver economically.

Maybe you see your business in one of these categories or the hundreds of other scenarios where a business just will not work. If this is you, what now?

Determining If You Should Abandon the Dream

This is the toughest part of this book, and the opposite of the hope and desire of running a successful business. But, you may be facing a grown-up moment here, and hiding from this reality is doing you a disservice. Most business owners eventually do have a difficult moment of reckoning.

Here are five critical questions to help you determine if you are at the stopping point for this business at this time.

1. *Can you make payroll?* If you do not have the money to make your next payroll, you have to stop. Now. Not paying employees is essentially stealing from them—stealing their time, at the very minimum. Don't cheat the people who are working to help you. They need to feed their families and pay their rent.

2. *Have you paid or can you pay your taxes?* If you haven't and can't pay your taxes, consider stopping your business now. Even in the worst-case scenario—bankruptcy—taxes are not dismissed in court. Every day you operate you build a higher mountain of tax debt—sales tax, payroll taxes, income taxes, licenses, and so on. It may be better to stop making the tax debt mountain higher.

3. *Realistically, in 30, 60, 90, or 180 days will the economics of your business be* much *better? Can the business support you and your family sustainably within the next year?* The allure of the idea of the business you love getting better in the future is undeniable. The world is full of stories of mythical businesses that "if only" they had operated longer, perhaps it would have succeeded. If you've been operating for six months or more, be honest with yourself. Will it really be much better in the next 90 or 180 days? Will it ever support you? Why? What would your fiercest critic say?

4. *Do you have the cash savings that will allow you to continue, and for how long?* If this doesn't work out, how broke will you be in 90 days? If you will be unable to make rent on your apartment next month, it is probably time to go to work for someone else and their business dream. At least then you'll have rent and groceries.

5. *Forget for a minute about how much you like your product or business. Will your customers buy enough of your product or services at a high enough price, often enough, to sustain the business and you?* This is a terribly hard question, as every business owner believes this to be true or they wouldn't have started the business in the first place. But, do your customers really like it as much as you do? If so, why aren't they already buying more, and why aren't they willing to pay more? Again, think of your fiercest critic and what they would say.

If You Decide to Stop

Finally, if you determine it is time to stop, focus on the pride of the accomplishment of starting a business, not the despair or sadness of the end. You are one of the few with the courage and bravery to actually go try.

Bravo, well done. You've done something most people are unwilling to tackle. Now all you have to do is figure out what comes next.

Maybe with a bit of time, you'll have another business idea and take the great leap. The next time, you'll be smarter, more experienced, improving your odds of success.

Notes

Chapter 1

1 https://en.wikipedia.org/wiki/Walter_Annenberg.

Chapter 3

1 https://en.wikipedia.org/wiki/The_Law_of_Success.
2 https://www.paychex.com/articles/payroll-taxes/avoid-payroll-mistakes.
3 https://www.getorderly.com/blog/your-ideal-cogs.
4 https://slowflowersjournal.com/breaking-it-down-pricing-advice-for-every-floral-designer/.

Chapter 4

1 https://en.wikipedia.org/wiki/Vilfredo_Pareto.

Chapter 5

1 https://blogs.findlaw.com/law_and_life/2014/10/who-legally-owns-your-facebook-posts.html.
2 https://www.businessinsider.com/amazon-jeff-bezos-chose-company-name-2018-5.

3 https://www.fastcompany.com/40494777/here-come-the-copyright-robots-for-hire-with-lawyers-in-tow.
4 https://heimdalsecurity.com/blog/ransomware-payouts/.
5 https://searchengineland.com/3-things-major-google-algorithm-update-260828#.
6 https://www.inquirer.com/business/small-business-website-sued-suits-ada-20200211.html.
7 https://support.google.com/business/answer/3038177/#Categories&zippy=%2Clearn-more.
8 https://www.localvisibilitysystem.com/?s=my+business+categories.
9 https://www.wordstream.com/blog/ws/2017/06/27/most-expensive-keywords.

Chapter 6

1 https://en.wikipedia.org/wiki/Joe_Girard.

Chapter 7

1 Joe Girard, *Joe Girard's 13 Essential Rules of Selling: How to Be a Top Achiever and Lead a Great Life* (McGraw-Hill, 2013).
2 https://www.illinoistrialpractice.com/2009/03/find-examples-of-bad-legal-writing-in-the-legalese-hall-of-shame.html.
3 Bill Schley, *The Micro-Script Rules: It's Not What People Hear. It's What They Repeat ...* (WidenerBooks, 2010).
4 https://kanbanize.com/lean-management/improvement/gemba-walk.

Chapter 8

1 I say "those days" because now the economics of dealerships has changed. They make more money on financing than they do on the car! They now frown on cash buyers.
2 https://en.wikipedia.org/wiki/Harvey_Mackay.
3 https://www.forbes.com/sites/forbesleadershipforum/2011/08/08/whats-a-lifetime-customer-worth-youd-better-know/?sh=3c80284d4cf1.
4 https://www.forbes.com/sites/micahsolomon/2013/09/18/empowered-employees-vs-brand-standards-the-customer-experience-needs-both/?sh=605ad195b8df.

Chapter 10

1 https://www.gutenberg.org/files/34258/34258-h/34258-h.htm.

Chapter 11

1 https://blog.hootsuite.com/facebook-secret-groups/.
2 https://www.washingtonpost.com/news/the-intersect/wp/2016/08/19/98-personal-data-points-that-facebook-uses-to-target-ads-to-you/.
3 https://www.komando.com/social-media/facebooks-52000-data-points-on-each-person-reveal-something-shocking-about-its-future/489188/#:~:text=Facebook's%2052%2C000%20data%20points%20on,about%20its%20future%20%2D%20Komando.com.
4 https://www.therichest.com/luxury/apartments-most-expensive-in-the-world/.
5 https://www.searchenginejournal.com/seo-101/meet-search-engines/#close.
6 https://sproutsocial.com/insights/new-social-media-demographics/.
7 https://sproutsocial.com/social-media-management/.
8 https://www.skyword.com/contentstandard/why-likes-dont-matter-for-engagement-metrics/.

Chapter 12

1 https://www.google.com/alerts.

Chapter 13

1 https://en.wikipedia.org/wiki/June_Martino.
2 Mark Sanborn, *The Fred Factor: How Passion in Your Work and Life Can Turn the Ordinary into the Extraordinary* (Currency, 2004) and *You Don't Need a Title to Be a Leader: How Anyone, Anywhere, Can Make a Positive Difference* (WaterBrook Press, 2006).
3 Angela Duckworth, *Grit: The Power of Passion and Perseverence* (Scribner, 2018).
4 Adam Grant, *Give and Take: Why Helping Others Drives Our Success*, reprint ed. (Penguin Books, 2014).
5 https://www.goodreads.com/quotes/5367145-it-is-said-that-there-are-four-kinds-of-horses.

Chapter 14

1 Robert Cialdini, *Influence: Science and Practice* (William Morrow & Company 1984).
2 Keith Cunningham, *The Road Less Stupid: Advice from the Chairman of the Board* (Keys to the Vault, 2018).
3 https://jamesclear.com/vince-lombardi-fundamentals.
4 https://savingplaces.org/stories/9-ways-people-are-supporting-small-businesses-during-the-coronavirus#.YGbS0mRufBs.
5 https://www.nytimes.com/2016/08/17/sports/olympics/nikki-hamblin-abbey-dagostino-womens-5000.html.
6 https://quoteinvestigator.com/2013/12/09/safe-harbor/#more-7781.

Epilogue

1 https://fortunly.com/blog/what-percentage-of-small-businesses-fail/.

Acknowledgments

An Undertaking of this magnitude takes months, even years, to complete. And if I am being honest, writing a book was never on my radar. Running a company the size and complexity of Deluxe is a large enough undertaking on its own. But when the good people at John Wiley & Sons approached me in November of 2019, I saw the wisdom of sharing the more than 100 years of knowledge Deluxe has accumulated in the small-business field.

There are so many people to thank who have helped bring this book to you. I'll start with my family and my beautiful and savvy wife, Jean Ann, herself a former Fortune 50 divisional chief financial officer, and daughter of a small-town hardware store owner. She understands the demands I face and the demands of small-businesspeople too. Our three children, Will, Matt, and Katie, join Jean Ann in passionately supporting me and the transformation of Deluxe. Being a "Deluxer" is a family affair at our house. Without their unwavering support, I could not lead Deluxe, nor be in a position to share the company's collective wisdom with you here.

Without the support of our board of directors, and our chair Cheryl Mayberry-McKissisk, I wouldn't have the privilege of leading Deluxe. I'm grateful for their support.

Amanda Brinkman, the visionary behind the *Small Business Revolution*, has been a generous and engaged partner throughout the many months it took to research this book. Her dedication and fortitude in promoting small businesses, to sharing their incredible stories, and to bringing the *Small Business Revolution* to millions of people across the country has been nothing less than remarkable. Being able to share even a small handful of examples from the television show has made this book all the more compelling.

Over the past 106 years, literally thousands of "Deluxers," have helped small businesses grow and evolve. We have done so directly with small-business owners, and indirectly through our thousands of banking clients who make connections with incredible business owners each and every day. I wish I could thank all of the many Deluxe employees who have impacted small businesses over the years, but that list would take pages and pages.

In particular, I want to acknowledge the incredible team that contributed their knowledge and expertise to the pages of this book: Andrew Neikamp, Julie Gordon, Tom Riccio, Devon Block, Jorge Carvalho, Gino Cardenas, Mark Byers, Brian Pfiefer, Wimbish Potter, Tamara Welter, Allison Checco, Susan Mays, Ben Gardner, Dan Flood, Tomasz Borowiecki, Jane Elliott, Amanda Parrilli, and Jeff Cotter.

Special thanks go to Jonathan Rozek, who brought his immense talent for capturing insights, writing, editing, and guidance to this project, transforming our years of knowledge into a comprehensive guide. And to Jennifer Amundson on our Deluxe team, who coordinated dozens of hours of interviews and provided her own insight into the pages of this book.

The publishing and editorial team at Wiley, specifically Mike Campbell, have been invaluable partners throughout this process, providing me with the time it took to do this right and the expertise to ensure we brought forth the kind of book that will help millions of small-businesses owners.

Special thanks to our partners at Flow Studios, who have been with us since day one filming *Small Business Revolution*. Their direction, storytelling, and adherence to detail are second to none and they have helped bring these incredible stories of perseverance, heroism, and struggle to millions of people.

Lastly, I want to thank Cameron Potts, an incredibly talented communications executive who shepherded this project from start to finish. He not only provided his writing and editing expertise and thoughtful anecdotes of small-business insight, but also guidance in keeping the project moving forward and navigating the many twists and turns that come with anything of this magnitude. His counsel and thoughtful leadership have been invaluable to this project, and without him this project would not have even been possible.

About the Author

BARRY C. MCCARTHY is president and chief executive officer of Deluxe (NYSE: DLX). Barry became the ninth CEO in the company's 106-year history on November 26, 2018. He is transforming the company from a legacy check printer into a modern, Trusted Payments and Business Technology™ company that helps businesses pay, get paid, optimize, and grow. Deluxe is a Fortune 1000 company, and its software and treasury solutions process more than $2.8 trillion in payments annually, nearly 15 percent of the U.S. economy.

In his first year, Barry delivered record revenue and 30 percent stock appreciation. He built a new leadership team, drove culture change by making every employee a shareholder, reinvigorated core values, and resegmented the company into four new operating units. He led the integration of 50-plus previous acquisitions and built a sales engine delivering the company's first successive quarters of sales-driven growth in more than a decade (excluding COVID impacts). He also established the company's first-ever Employee Resource Groups (ERGs) and made substantial human and financial capital commitments to fight racism. He navigated the company through the COVID crisis while expanding margins and lowering net debt to the lowest level in more than two years.

Prior to joining Deluxe, he spent 14 years at First Data (formerly NYSE: FDC, now part of Fiserv, NASDAQ: FISV), running most businesses globally. He was the only senior executive to survive and thrive from the historic KKR-led LBO to its IPO nearly a decade later, serving seven CEOs.

Barry has a track record of delivering innovative tech-enabled solutions. He led the historic First Data–Apple collaboration supporting ApplePay, and with Google on Google Wallet and Android Pay. He created the best-selling First Data–branded credit card terminals generating over $2 billion in revenue. At Verisign (NASDAQ: VRSN), he repositioned and grew their payments business, leading to its acquisition by PayPal. He co-founded, built, and sold MagnaCash, a Silicon Valley micropayments company that worked like today's iTunes checkout. Earlier he ran the Wells Fargo ATM/Debit business delivering the world's first web-enabled ATM network and personalized UI/UX. Barry was also nonexecutive chairman of eSurg.com, a venture-backed online medical supply start-up acquired by market leader Henry Schein (NASDAQ: HSIC).

He began his career and spent 12 years at Procter & Gamble in roles of increasing responsibility in sales, product, and brand marketing, where he launched of dozens of new products.

Barry serves on the Boards of the National Urban League, Minneapolis Business Partnership, Metro Atlanta Chamber, Carter Center, and Woodruff Arts Center. He was the inaugural Chair of FinTech-Atlanta, and Chair of Technology Association of Georgia (TAG). He served on the Boards of Bank of America Merchant Services (NY), PNC Merchant Services (Pittsburg), Standard Chartered Merchant Services (Singapore), American Transaction Processors Coalition (Atlanta), Payments 20 (London/Atlanta), Junior Achievement of Georgia, and Catholic Charities of Atlanta, where he founded the Youth Leadership Fellows program.

He earned an MBA from the Kellogg School of Management at Northwestern University.

Index

223